FROM JUNE - 19

Beyond Acceptance

Beyond Acceptance

Parents of Lesbians and Gays Talk About Their Experiences

Carolyn Welch Griffin
Marian J. Wirth
Arthur G. Wirth

Prentice-Hall, Inc.
Englewood Cliffs, New Jersey

Prentice-Hall International, Inc., *London*
Prentice-Hall of Australia, Pty. Ltd., *Sydney*
Prentice-Hall Canada, Inc., *Toronto*
Prentice-Hall of India Private Ltd., *New Delhi*
Prentice-Hall of Southeast Asia Pte. Ltd., *Singapore*
Whitehall Books, Ltd., Wellington, *New Zealand*
Editora Prentice-Hall do Brasil Ltda., *Rio de Janeiro*
Prentice-Hall Hispanoamericana, S.A., *Mexico*

© 1986 *by*

PRENTICE-HALL, INC.
Englewood Cliffs, N.J.

Library of Congress Cataloging-in-Publication Data

Griffin, Carolyn Welch,
    Beyond acceptance.

    Bibliography: p
    Includes index.
    1. Homosexuality—United States. 2. Homosexuals—
United States—Family relationships. 3. Parent
and child—United States. I. Wirth, Marian Jenks,
        . II. Wirth, Arthur G.,
III. Title.
HQ76.3.U5G75 1986 306.7'66'0973   86-267

ISBN 0-13-075938-4

Printed in the United States of America

We were learners. We learned most from our own gay children, our families, and from the parents who let us record their words. Their willingness to share recollections of the journey that took them to acceptance and beyond, made it possible for us to bring this book into being.

Contents

Foreword

It is about a dozen years since parents began meeting in groups across the nation. When we first got together, it was for the purpose of bringing support and comfort to one another. We told our family histories and shared our feelings and experiences. What evolved was the realization that our gay sons and lesbian daughters were not a problem; that the problem was a very misinformed society.

Our observations have helped us to understand gay persons. We have learned that for about ten percent of the population it is natural to be attracted to the same sex; that there really is no choice in one's sexuality; and that there is no pattern to the kind of family that has a gay child. The love we had for our children sustained us while we learned.

Today there are more than seventy-five parent groups, about another twenty-five in formation, and some sixty-five additional parent contacts in as many towns and cities nationwide. Because our children are victims of a great deal of misinformation, we are trying to change attitudes towards them by speaking out and by sharing with you—our community-at-large—what we have learned.

This is what the authors of *Beyond Acceptance* have accomplished. They have invited you into their lives through interviews with parents and others in their local parent group, through their rap and discussion meetings, and by sharing their thoughts and experiences. They have written about their group so you can observe the stages that so many of us parents have gone through.

Each parent group is unique, yet each is the same. The group represented in this book is in the heartland of America. It speaks for all of us. It gets to the heart of the parents' movement.

When I first became involved eleven years ago, I had hopes that we would put ourselves out of business in a few years. It is still my hope, but as long as we are needed we will be available. That's for sure!

Adele Starr, President
Federation of Parents and Friends
of Lesbians and Gays (Parents FLAG)

Introduction

This is a story from parents of lesbian and gay children. More specifically, it is a report of the experiences of twenty-three parents who worked together over a period of years in a self-help organization called Parents and Friends of Lesbians and Gays (Parents FLAG).* The authors and others in the group have wrestled with the personal and cultural implications of the fact that we are parents of gay or lesbian adult children. We have been moved by the varieties of pain that we and our children have suffered. We have been equally moved by the varieties of growth that emerged as, together, we confronted our common experience. Our need to report grew out of our own awareness of changes taking place in us personally and in others in the group.

Because our society rejects gay people, most parents of lesbians and gays will experience some of the varieties of pain we have known. We realize that parents who discover that someone in their family is gay often feel terribly isolated. It can be a great relief to learn that they are not alone.

We also want to share the varieties of personal and family growth that we have seen in our group. We make no claims for smooth transition from pain to enlightenment, but we know that our tranformations have been real. Our changes are not fixed; we are very much aware that we too are "in process."

The group members interviewed were white, middle-class Americans from a large Midwestern metropolitan area. They were from widely differing vocational, educational, and religious backgrounds, with ages ranging from forty to seventy.

As in any self-help group, members of Parents FLAG join for varying periods of time. Our direct quotes are based on interviews with parents who joined the group and stayed in for

---

*Parents FLAG is a national network of scores of self-help groups from all parts of the United States. The address of the national headquarters is Box 24565, Los Angeles, CA 90024.

a considerable length of time. In this sense, the group we interviewed was self-selected. Names and places have been changed to preserve privacy. We are not social scientists, but have read many studies about gay people in America. Our understanding has been significantly broadened by our reading as well as by our experiences. We draw on both in commenting on what we have learned that may be helpful to other parents of lesbian or gay children.

ON TERMINOLOGY

Homosexuality is a varied and complex phenomenon. There are, for example, many people who have experienced homosexual incidents. These have not affected their heterosexual orientation. There are others who are bisexual. In this book, our remarks refer primarily to that category of sexuality which characterizes most of the gay or lesbian children of parents in our group. Our childrens' orientation is primarily or exclusively homosexual. They have no more inclination to change their sexual orientation than do those of us who are exclusively heterosexual.

As we consider the terms homosexual or gay to be interchangeable, a brief comment on the term gay is in order. There seems to be no single, simple account of its origins. Gay people themselves prefer to be called gay rather than homosexual. To many gay people the word homosexual emphasizes only the sexual aspect of their lives, while gay refers to the entire range of their human relationships. It also indicates the positive feelings they have about their sexual orientation. Because homosexual is a word in general usage, however, we will from time to time use it as an alternative to gay. Many women in the gay community prefer to be called lesbian, therefore, we will often use the term "gay men and lesbians," although we will use gay occasionally as the umbrella term.

Heterosexism is a word that is moving into common usage. Like the words racism, sexism, ageism or classism, it refers to the idea that one group—in this case heterosexuals—

is superior and only that group is truly acceptable. With all of these terms there is an implicit requirement by the "superior" group that those in the secondary group "stay in their place." They should not have the same privileges or rights. They should not in any way disturb those in power, nor challenge the written or unwritten rules. If they do, the majority feels justified in punishing and ostracizing those who are different.

Another word of recent origin that we use is homophobia. This word comes from George Weinberg's book, *Society and the Healthy Homosexual.* It means an irrational and excessive fear of lesbians and gay men which often leads to hate and even violence. Homophobia is pervasive throughout our culture, and it is this fear that must be countered. We hope this book will make a contribution to removing the fear.

Carolyn Welch Griffin
Marian J. Wirth
Arthur G. Wirth

Acknowledgments

We wish to acknowledge permission from the following publishers to quote from copyrighted materials cited in the text: Dignity, Inc.; Friends Book Center; Indiana University Press; Jubilee, Inc.; The Pilgrim Press; Sage Publications, Inc.; and Redwood Records. We would also like to thank Methodist Bishop Melvin Wheatley (ret.) who permitted us to quote from an address he delivered.

Many people helped and encouraged us in various stages of the writing. We owe a special debt of gratitude to Robin Griffin who typed endless transcripts of interviews, to Betty Torstrick for her care and accuracy in preparing the final draft of the manuscript, and to Jim Thomas for his insightful editorial advice.

Beyond Acceptance

chapter 1

Finding Out

As the truth replaces fear and superstition, attitudes are changing. In the meantime, don't let society rob you of your special child.[1]

The moment when our children chose to tell us of their homosexuality was a moment of shock and pain. Our lives were placed on a different course. Years do not erase the details of the day. We recall the weather, the time of day, the room, our thoughts, and most of all, our feelings. It was a moment that marked the beginning of a journey through a powerful grief.

It happened on a Sunday morning—a sunny day in February. We were still in bed when Craig came into the room and said, "I have something I want to tell you."

He sat at the foot of the bed, crossed his arms, and I thought, "Oh my God." Then he said, "I can't lie to you anymore. I'm gay."

The words made my ears ring. We argued, and there was some uproar. I begged him not to act on it, but he already had. It was a bad scene for a while. Later, after I quieted down, I had a feeling that was about the same as when somebody dies. For a long time I went around with a lump in my throat.

We were all sitting around our daughter's living room, with a Christmas tree in the corner—a regular family gathering. Chris said he had something to tell us, and then he hemmed and hawed for what seemed like five minutes. He said things like, "I don't know how to tell you this," and, "This may be hard to hear."

If I had it to do over again, I would have helped him by saying, "Are you trying to tell us you're gay?" But at that time, I didn't consciously admit to myself that I had any idea of what was coming. I think I did know, down deep somewhere, but I just wanted to postpone what I perceived as difficult news, if even for a few minutes.

Finally, Chris said something about the fact that he was attracted to men. Since Jack and I had had some suspicions in the past because Chris hadn't dated, it wasn't a complete shock.

I remember thinking, "Well, this is it. The die is cast, and what we feared has come to pass." I was disappointed, but the full effect didn't hit me until later.

I knew I should support Chris' decision, and I did. I just put all the worries about my feelings on hold.

Our daughter sent my wife and me a letter to tell us. She said she chose this method because she wanted to think out her thoughts very carefully. I think she told us very diplomatically. She wrote that being a lesbian was important in her life and that she had to share it with us. She then asked for our response.

My wife and I felt like our world had come to an end. We hit the depths of our emotions. We had guilt feelings and thought that everything we had done with our children was wrong. For a brief time, we even thought about mutual suicide.

Nancy and Paul had a special problem with their son, Tim, who is totally deaf. Both parents had spent long hours helping with Tim's education. They are a close and caring family.

Nancy: *When we first found out, it was very traumatic.*
Paul: *Tim had been having a terrible time emotionally. The deaf are very emotional people anyway, because they have a harder time expressing themselves than do hearing persons. He had been throwing temper tantrums.*

Nancy: *We had at least a year and a half that was rough before we found out.*

Paul: *He didn't know how to cope with it. He didn't know how to tell us.*

Nancy: *We didn't know what to do. We were walking on eggs, trying not to say anything wrong because he was so keyed up. We found out later he had discussed being gay with his older brother who told him it was just a phase. That didn't help, and finally he had even thought of killing himself.*

Paul: *We weren't fighting him. We were trying to help him. But we didn't know how to protect him. We had no idea that he was so upset because he was gay.*

Nancy: *We told him we were trying to help him cope with what was bothering him. He kept saying, "You don't understand. You just don't understand." I said, "No, we don't understand you, but we're trying to."*

Paul: *Then one morning about three o'clock, he woke us up and told us his truck had been stolen. It was a fancy pick-up truck, and he told us it had been taken on the east side—a bar area. Boy, did he hate to tell us about that robbery. I said, "My God, what were you doing over on the east side? You know you're not supposed to be over there!" I went back to bed, because I was tired and a bit disgusted.*

Nancy: *Tim and I stayed up and were sitting at the kitchen table. And I said, "Tim, I just can't imagine your being stupid enough to be over there on the east side. You know what goes on over there."*

Then he looked at me and said, "I'm gay. That's why I was there."

And with that I said, "I knew something was wrong, but I didn't know what. I thought you were over there fooling around with whores."

Right away we started talking. He said, "I don't want to be that way, Mother, but I am."

I said, "Who got to you?"

He said, "Nobody."

I said, "Don't tell me that. I know somebody got to you."

He said, "No, Mother. To this day, no one has ever approached me."

After that we just talked about it. It was a rough period. I said to Paul the next day, "I told you I knew something terrible was wrong. It's not a whore. He's a homosexual. Oh my God, Paul, what will we do?"

Paul: *We discussed things and decided we'd better take him to a psychiatrist. We thought surely a psychiatrist could straighten him out. We didn't think he had to be gay. We thought he was confused. Well we found out he wasn't.*

One day at work I saw a letter from Marsha on my desk. I got this funny feeling in the pit of my stomach. I knew it was going to be something bad; so I quickly went to the ladies' lounge to open the letter.

Instead, it was just a nice long letter saying she'd like to talk to me alone, and would I come get her at the college where she was a student. I drove up to get her. When we started home, Marsha asked to drive. I thought, "My goodness! She never wants to do that."

We hadn't gone far when she started talking. She said, "I know you're wondering why I wanted to talk to you alone. I don't know whether you've suspected it or not, but I'm gay."

I said, "Well, yes, I have suspected it." I continued talking to keep from crying and sobbing and screaming. I didn't cry in front of her. I'll put it that way.

We had a nice, long talk all the way home. She asked me if she should tell her dad that weekend. I felt that we ought to wait a little while and let me adjust first, because I figured we'd have to pick her dad up off the floor or the ceiling or somewhere and take him to the hospital.

For a few days, this mother handled her feelings alone. She felt that she had to protect her husband. Her unshared grief finally boiled over, and she told her husband during a family argument.

I didn't find out from Marsha. I found out from my wife. Marsha had talked with her earlier. Ruth and I were having a family spat when she said something to the effect that on top of all the other problems we had, we also had to deal with the fact that we had a daughter who was homosexual. Everything stopped right there.

I was bewildered. I was hurt by the fact that my daughter didn't trust me enough to tell me. I was very disappointed and began wondering just how shallow our relationship had been. Where had I failed? Why was she afraid of me? Where had I gone wrong in raising her so that she didn't feel secure in talking to me? My first resolve was not so much to talk to her about being gay, but to talk about our relationship.

I thought about it awhile and decided I had to have open communication with Marsha. I wrote her a letter and told her that I didn't understand all of it; that I had questions I wanted to discuss privately. I felt pleased that I had established a line of communication with her.

Don came out to me after another son let it slip that he was gay. I have four sons and a daughter. My other boys had been talking about Don and his "queer" friends. When I objected to the way they were talking, one said, "Well, Mom, you know Don's gay."

I said, "Don't say that about him. After all, he's your brother." I became very defensive and talked about it being okay that Don was not an athlete. I started to cry. I said, "I don't know why I'm crying. I don't believe this. I don't think it's true." A little while later, the phone rang.

One of my other sons had called Don and told him, "You'd better call Mother. We just told her you're gay. She's all upset."

My first question when Don called was, "Don, are you gay?" And he said, "Yes, but you've always known that." I said, "When did you find out?" He answered, "When I was about three or four."

I felt that I had failed. I thought, "How am I going to deal with this? What will the neighbors say?" I had a lot of bad information stored in the back of my head.

It's a blow to your ego to think you're such a competent and perceptive parent and then find you have a gay child. You think you know your child so well and then find out he knew this at a young age and didn't tell. You feel you really missed the boat in some things.

Sometimes parents sense what their child is about to tell them. Inadvertently, they give their child a double message, "Tell me, but don't tell me." Most of us want to hold back the news.

Sarah tried to tell us over the phone. She began to cry. I told her I knew something was seriously wrong. I had had thoughts that she might be lesbian, but I kept pushing them out of my mind. I told her to call back whenever she thought she could talk.

I didn't really want to hear it. I probably could have helped by saying, "Sarah, are you trying to tell us you're gay?" But I was afraid she'd say "yes." And I wasn't about to take a chance on that.

It was about three days later when we got the letter, and I didn't even want to open it. It was a loving letter, a caring letter. She told us she had been aware of her gayness since she was twelve. She wasn't ashamed of it. She had found somebody she loved who loved her. For the first time in her life she wasn't lonely anymore.

Herb and I cried when we read the letter because it was full of pain. It's a letter no parent wants to receive. Then we thought, "Where do we go from here?"

THE PARADOX: PAIN AND SORROW VERSUS FREEDOM AND FULFILLMENT

All of us, by the time we have reached the middle years, have had a full share of disillusionment and disappointment. We have learned that the enchanting folk tales of our childhood have no literal truth. Cinderella has a fifty-percent chance of ending in the divorce courts, frogs don't change into princes, and ugly ducklings usually grow up to be ugly ducks. If we are lucky, we learn to accept reality, roll with the punches, and become philosophical about our disappointments.

Yet there is a special poignancy where shattered expectations about our children are concerned. One compensation for life's bruises is that our children will "do us honor." We have given them love and made sacrifices for them. In return, consciously or unconsciously, we expect our children to make up for the past, enrich the present, and represent the future. We think they will accomplish great things, bring us the joy of happy marriages, and give us grandchildren.

Few experiences cause us to realize the folly of these unrealistic expectations as quickly or as effectively as learning that one of our children is gay. Our grief is intense, and we have trouble giving it a name because it touches every phase of our lives. Often, it is likened to having a death in the family.

And there *is* a death—of the familiar beliefs and hopes that have kept us going through our child-raising years.

Unaware of any alternatives, we grieve as our self-worth is threatened. We think, "My child is sick, I am sick, our family life is sick. I hurt my baby." A feeling of horror comes over us as we often admit to ourselves, "I do not approve of what my child is. He or she is strange, weird, perverted. I'm not sure I want to be around people like that." Remorse and tears can become our daily companions as we are caught by the opinions which fill the libraries and the airwaves. No one really knows, yet everyone thinks he or she knows. Even so-called experts tell us opposite ideas about cause, "cure," life style, and even what homosexuality is. We experience an emotional loss.

I thought, "Oh my God. My daughter is a pervert!" I felt that I was the world's biggest failure. Every father I saw was better than I was.

Every book that I had seen said homosexuality was caused by a disturbance in the family. They said that there was usually an absent or rejecting father and a domineering, seductive, or binding kind of mother. I thought about how much Jack worked when the kids were small and the fact that I was the one who stayed home and took care of them. I twisted it all around and said, "Yes, maybe we are like that. Maybe there was something really wrong with us."

We grieve in our churches as we listen to the religious attacks against our children. We wonder if our child is living sinfully, and we fear for his or her salvation. We hear our religious leaders speak out against homosexuality and find ourselves in distress as unthinking church members voice unkind thoughts. We experience a spiritual loss.

Right after we found out about our gay daughter, our church began exploring the idea of openly accepting gays and lesbians. I found it hard to sit near people who were saying, "We shouldn't have to vote on that." Some of the members even passed around a petition to keep lesbians and gays out of the church. That was hard to handle. I'd come home from church and scream and yell that if those were the kind of people God wanted in his church, then God didn't need me.

We grieve over the loss of grandchildren. It does not matter that some of us will have grandchildren from our other children. We want them from each of our children. Our name, our genes, will not be carried on by our gay child. Many of us know this feeling is self-centered, but that does not lessen it. This desire is so basic that few parents escape the yearning. It is almost universal. We do not, as yet, know that many gay people do have children. The loss we feel could be called a biological loss.

I've always loved babies and kids. One of my first thoughts was that Mary will never bring home a nice young man and say, "This is it, Mom. This is the man I love." I'll never have grandkids from Mary. She'll never have a child that I can think of as her child.

I've had dreams of a successful family with my three children going out and getting married and having their own children. I'd have all these grandchildren to play with. All at once, one-third of my trio goes off on a tangent.

We grieve over our loss of status as we are faced with unfamiliar shame. We have an uneasy feeling, as we become aware that we are associated with an "undesirable" group. We fear that anger and rejection will be directed toward us when people learn we have a gay or lesbian child. We are confused about how to treat our child's partner, and we do not know how our child will fit into our everyday life. We are worried about the effect on our other children and grandchildren, our parents and siblings, our friends, our neighbors, the people we work with. This is a social loss.

My husband doesn't want his family to know. To me that means he's ashamed of Mary. But, I myself hesitate. I'd like to tell my good friend. We grew up together, and I would like for her to know. But I don't know what she would think of me or Mary. She makes a lot of negative comments about gays.

And we usually experience our multiple loss alone. We have to go about our lives with a secret pain that we cannot share. We cannot often hear consoling words from our friends. It is understandable that parents often describe their reactions in such highly charged terms as: failure, fright, disappointment, shame, and guilt. Occasionally, parents will say that it would be easier to handle the death of a child than having a gay child. While this reaction does not usually last, it is a painful example of how damaging homophobia is in our society. The reason for such intense feelings may be that the normal death of a child carries no shame, while having a gay child is seen as bringing lifelong dishonor to the family.

Sooner or later, however, parents have to go beyond the cultural messages of rejection and hatred if they are to feel any peace. Facing the problem may cost us a great deal of time and pain. It is frightening to let go of established guideposts when there are only shaky and unproven ones to replace them. And there is usually little help from any of the traditional sources such as church, social groups, extended family, or even close friends. Parents must sink or swim by their own efforts.

But swim many of them do. The decision to go against hurtful societal views often does more than just help them survive. The act of confronting homosexuality openly and courageously can become a source of freedom and fulfillment in the family. It can strengthen affection between the parents and the child. It can begin a movement towards restoring the wholeness of everyone involved.

We know that some parents may choose to remain caught in despondency. This exacts its own high cost. These parents take on the prejudices of the culture and do damage to themselves. By refusing to get involved in the struggle to change their inaccurate perceptions, they never stop struggling.

But a move to a positive view is not easy. The glimmer of the "up" feelings is often countered by the "down" messages regularly heard in day-to-day interactions. Parents have often referred to this experience as similar to being on a roller coaster, with its sudden unpredictable ups and downs.

With time and effort, though, the balance can be tipped toward a positive experience. More independent thinking and a sense of personal power are often reported.

INITIAL PARENTAL ACTIONS

Before exploring features of the road to a positive resolution, it is useful to identify some of the ways that parents react immediately after finding out. There are four actions that parents may take that are typical. The first three lead to parental despair; the fourth opens possibilities for change and, eventually, inner peace. They are: breaking contact, trying to change the child, ignoring the issue, and accepting reality.

Breaking Contact

There are some parents who choose to cast out the gay child completely. We have met many such children. They look at us with longing and puzzlement, wondering why it is that we can accept them and their parents cannot.

When I was thirteen, there was a boy in junior high with me whom I liked a lot. In fact, I was in love with him. My sexual feeling for him scared me, but still that was how I felt. He was in an automobile accident, and for a while I thought he might die. I often cried because he meant so much to me. There was nothing sexual between us.

My mother noticed how unhappy I was and kept asking what was wrong. We had always been close so I finally got up the nerve to tell her that I was gay. She got upset and threw me out. She said she wasn't going to let me hurt my younger brother and sisters.

I didn't know what to do. I got some of my clothes and left. My dad was coming up the walk as I was leaving. He wasn't too upset. He just said, "You know how your mother is," and went inside.

I went to a massage parlor I had heard of and asked for a job. They were nice to me and even let me sleep there. I got the job, and I have been working there for five years now. I don't know what I would have done if they hadn't helped me out. I don't go to school anymore, but I'm making loads of money. I have more money than any kid my age that I know.

But I miss my family. Sometimes I walk up and down the street hoping my mom will let me in. Once she came out and told me that when the kids get bigger, I could visit, but so far I haven't been able to go in. Sometimes I go near where my dad works and see him when he goes out to lunch. He shakes my hand and says, "How's it going?" But he doesn't ask me to come home either. Someday maybe my parents will take me back. I keep hoping.

David is lucky. He still lives. He still has hope. Experts tell us that many "throw-away" children die tragically, alone, with no one to care. There is an unknown toll of rejected gay children who become victims of the seamy side of street life—drug addiction, prostitution, and crime.

Parents who cut off their relationship with their child pay a heavy price. They can push their son or daughter out of their lives, but not out of their hearts. They have to expend a great deal of energy maintaining a façade as they go about their daily routine. Weighed down with guilt, anger, and disappointment, they are confined to a life without their children.

Punishing the victim never solves the problem—and our gay and lesbian children have become the victims of a vast array of false information and prejudicial treatment.

Trying to Change the Child

A large number of parents focus their energies on strategies to change their children. Recent research holds that fundamental sexual orientation does not change. Still, there are three ways in which parents pursue false hopes: taking the child to a psychotherapist, leading the child to religious conversion, and/or encouraging the child to have a sexual relationship with a person of the opposite sex.

Taking the Child to a Psychotherapist. Psychotherapy as a source for the change of a person's sexual orientation is often one of the first ideas a parent considers. Thinking of a child's homosexual orientation as an illness draws parents towards the idea of a medical cure.

One couple decided to take their son to a psychiatrist when they first learned that he was gay. The psychiatrist said he could cure their son if their bank account were large enough, and asked to see their bank statement. He told them they would have to spend several thousand dollars. This unethical behavior created guilt for the parents, as they were not wealthy enough to afford his services. Fortunately, this couple learned that the psychiatrist could not support his claim, and they did not fall victim to the sham. The most that health care professionals can do is help families learn to accept the homosexual member in a constructive way. A growing number of knowledgeable, responsible therapists are committed to supporting such a goal.

Leading the Child to Religious Conversion. Some parents look to their religion as a way of getting their children into a heterosexual life style. Our gay and lesbian children, however, have for years attended houses of worship hearing of the love of God for all except themselves. They have come to an awareness of their homosexuality slowly and usually painfully, never casually. Many report feeling desolation and bewilderment as they became aware of being attracted to members of their own sex. Often they prayed and hoped for a change from God. At times they considered suicide as the only way out. Some wanted to be what they were hearing in the churches that they should be, and yet they knew they could not be. Others denied who they were for years, even decades.

Often, religious leaders themselves are poorly informed about the biological and social aspects of homosexuality. Frequently they do not acknowledge that there are widely differing positions among religious leaders. They may not even be accurate about Biblical perspective and interpretation. Families can be ripped apart when they encounter such insensitivity and ignorance.

Religion may offer support and understanding, but it cannot alter sexual orientation.

Encouraging the Child to Have a Relationship with a Person of the Opposite Sex. Heterosexual expression is a familiar part of life. Many parents have been taught that this is the only natural way. They often hope and believe that a good sexual experience with someone of the opposite sex will turn their gay son or lesbian daughter around. The message to the gay person is, "Just give it a chance. You'll see how great my kind of love is, and everything will be just fine." What this often does is create heartache for both the gay person and for the partner who is being used in an experiment doomed to failure.

Parents who cling to the illusion that change can occur, whether in the name of Freud, God, or opposite-sex love, put themselves and their child through unnecessary anguish. It is an exercise in futility.

The next story tells about one young man who tried all the above ideas in order to change. He is still gay, but he and others are suffering from guilt and confusion. No one has any suggestions for him or for his family now. He has tried them all.

John is filled with guilt, depression and self-loathing. From early adolescence he has realized that he is gay. He has struggled against his nature—praying a lot and suffering in isolation. His father, now retired, was a minister who considered homosexuality to be a sinful choice.

Hoping a heterosexual relationship would change him, John married a young woman who was his friend. She was kind and understanding, went to his church, and was totally dedicated to him. They lived together for a year. It was a year of agony for him. Finally, he left her and secretly moved in with a man.

Buffeted by the punishing statements he heard, his move into the homosexual life style brought him no peace. In the hopes that he could feel sexually attracted to women, he went to a Christian psychologist and joined a religious group dedicated to changing gay men. Neither effort worked.

In desperation he confessed his secret life to his brother who thought it was his duty to inform the rest of the family. John's father took him to their present minister, and in an emotional session John confessed his "sin" and asked for forgiveness. He moved back in with his wife.

A year later the couple had a child who died from sudden infant death syndrome. John thinks God is punishing him for being gay. Most of the people in his church agree with him. John's wife is suffering a hell of her own. She cannot feel secure and wonders how long he will stay with her this time.

This couple is in misery because the husband is being forced to accept a life style into which he simply cannot fit. Their hopes for happiness are tied up in the idea that somehow John's sexual nature will change.

Our gay children are brave, strong, and searching. They are what they are. They will remain what they are. Acceptance by parents gives them a boost in coping with a tough world. Trying to change them adds enormously to their burden.

Ignoring the Issue: The Ostrich Effect

Another response which tempts parents is a decision to ignore the situation, yet still maintain contact. We also call this the ostrich effect. Small children, when fearful of thunderstorms, try to feel safe by crawling under the blankets and pulling the covers over their heads. "If we can't see it or hear it, maybe it will go away." Adults sometimes handle problems this same way. The child within needs to feel safe from fear, and the denial of the situation can be helpful for awhile. It gives some people time to absorb the information.

Some parents do not give up that denial system, and continue to say, "You've told me you're gay. I hope you know what you're doing. Don't talk about it with me anymore. I don't want to know about that part of your life. We'll keep everything else in our interactions like it was before."

The internal and external conflicts that absorb mothers and fathers in their early grief do not spontaneously disappear. These conflicts, left unchallenged, keep such parents precariously balanced. They cannot break off with their child.

Nor can they examine and revise their ideas which created the conflict. So they silently stay on this uncommitted course. In essence, they try to move back to a safer, earlier time when for them the problem of society's homophobia did not exist.

Children who experience this response sense the double bind the parents are feeling. Often they are caught in the same bind. Many want to sit down with their parents and teach them all they have learned. They want to share their joys and hurts, but they know they cannot bring up the subject. Issues surrounding homosexuality form a barrier that separates children from parents.

Mike's is a case in point. He loves his parents, and they love him. Being a teenager was hell for him as he became aware that he was gay. He took the extreme step of attempting suicide. Shaken by the experience, he began to turn himself around. Like so many lesbians and gays, he finally came to say, "I am a homosexual, a queer, a faggot. I've always heard it is bad to be one of 'them,' but I know that I'm okay. No one will convince me that I am not."

Mike now has a bedrock feeling of self-worth which led to the decision to tell his parents. The telling itself was calm and uneventful. But there was firm resistance to any follow-up. His sense of well-being gave him the courage to be a leader in the fight for gay rights. He tried often to share his activities with his parents, but they weren't interested. Mike attended family gatherings, but his life style was never mentioned. He listened to all the personal stories of his brothers, sisters, and cousins, but knew he could never speak of his own. He was excluded from equal participation in family life and was relegated to being a passive observer.

When Mike became an effective activist for gay rights, he was invited to appear on televison. One night, Mike dropped by his family home for a visit. His father came into the living room with a gun, pointed it at him, and said, "If I see you on television, I will kill you." Mike left, shaken and fearful. He did appear on TV.

A year has passed and the family has drifted back into the old routine. Mike visits, listens, doesn't speak about his own life, and wonders if his father could really hurt him. He feels that he is sitting on a volcano, but he says the greater tragedy for him is the determined silence with which his parents treat his life outside the family. Despite the fact that his family did not come through for him, he has continued his work for gay rights.

While the threat to Mike's life is extreme, less dramatic forms of the ostrich effect are very common and take their toll. Pushing away a part of life that is important never solves any problems. The problems haunt us when we are frightened and weak, and we find ourselves taking actions that later fill us with remorse. Our emotional responses can be held back only so long. For everyone concerned it is important that the ideas we have about homosexuality be carefully studied.

Accepting Reality

Fortunately, there is another response that any parent can choose to take—accepting reality. Such acceptance is a process that is often slow and uncomfortable. But for those who stay with it, the rewards are great. The people we interviewed are examples of those who chose this path.

On the surface, these parents appear to have little in common. Some are conservative, others liberal. Some are divorced or widowed, others have the traditional, two-parent family structure. Religious beliefs fall into a wide range, from being deeply and traditionally religious to being agnostic or atheist. Almost all felt negative about or aloof from gayness before they knew of their children's homosexuality.

There is a common thread shared by all. Our interviewed parents gave top priority to maintaining a good relationship with their children. As one father put it, "When I found out, I soon decided I had to either stand with my son or support the rejecting attitudes of the society. I chose to stand with my child."

Such parents often reported that they had a moment when they realized that this child of theirs, labeled a "social reject" is the same child they held in their arms as an infant. It is the child they nurtured through good times and bad, and who gave them love and trust. The basic decision they made then was to let nothing interfere with the caring relationship.

I told myself I didn't care how Dave, my husband, reacted. I didn't care what he did. There was nothing that would make me kick Carol out of the house. Never would I tell her she couldn't come to see us. There were many things that went through my mind. I wondered how I could know Carol's friends, how I could still be a part of her life.

Right after Steve told us, things were really bad. I remember one time when he wanted to go out and I wouldn't give him the car; but he was determined to go and meet this guy anyway. He dressed and left. I got in the car and was going to the store when I saw him walking down Main Street. I just felt terrible for him. Even though I was upset, I was feeling sorry for him too. I made a rule for myself that I wasn't going to browbeat him anymore or get him to conform to my rules. I wasn't going to do anything to hurt him again.

When I found out Don was gay, it was hard, certainly. But a day or two after I knew, I was sitting by myself and thought, "He's still the same son who asked me for five dollars this morning; he's the same boy who was here for breakfast, who took out the trash, who wrecked the car. His sexuality doesn't have anything to do with his integrity or his ability to love or his worth."

I guess I could have said, "Get out of my life and don't ever come back." And he could have agreed. But he wouldn't have been out of my life. I would have been the one to lose. I would have lost the things we have shared and all our closeness. He's a loving, honest, and wonderful son. He told me he was gay, and he's still a loving, honest, and wonderful son. I don't think you have to be anything but full of love to learn to accept your child.

These parents also realized a fundamental truth—their gay and lesbian children would not change. The prime area for change would have to be in their own attitudes and ideas. This started our parents on a challenging course. It required that they "unlearn" the myths of the culture and stand against them.

It was scary but freeing. Love for their children told them they were on the right path.

The rest of this book details the process that parents go through to accept their children and change their own attitudes. As part of this process, parents have to modify their internal belief system, learn the facts, confront the prevailing cultural view, and move to new levels of understanding. This often arduous course produces personal and familial changes of extraordinary value. These parents, with both gay and nongay children, develop an inner strength that allows all of them to confront life's challenges realistically.

NOTE FOR CHAPTER 1

[1]Adele Starr, statement in *About Our Children* (Los Angeles: Federation of Parents and Friends of Lesbians and Gays, Inc., 1978). (Pamplet available free, Box 24565, Los Angeles, CA 90024.)

chapter 2

What We Learned from Books

The negative feelings I had about homosexuality came from everything I had contact with as I was growing up: from my mother, from the kids in school, from outhouse and toilet walls, from books and magazines.

———————————

In my own growing up, I'm not sure how I managed to pick up only misinformation about gays. Yet how could it have been otherwise, as our society is rampantly homophobic? Until recent years, misinformation was the only game in town.

Parents today are in a situation somewhat analogous to the children of my generation. I grew up in the 1920s and 1930s. Sexual matters, even the simplest facts, like where babies came from, were regarded as dangerous. There was a conspiracy of silence.

These same children, now grown up and parents, have once again been victimized by a conspiracy of silence and have had to rely on gossip instead of guidance—this time concerning homosexuality.

———————————

Neither my husband nor I knew anything about homosexuality outside of the gutter language that we had heard. You know, queers

and fags and words like that. We simply didn't have enough informa-
tion to have done any independent thinking on the subject. But how
many of us do have information on homosexuality until it confronts us?

Armed with only myths, we, as parents of gay children, were poorly prepared to defend ourselves against the shock and confusion we felt at first. We had been victimized on several counts. We were hurt by the outdated, unsubstantiated and often opposing "expert" opinions that floated around in the scientific community. We were hurt by the whispers, smirks, innuendoes and jokes that were an acceptable part of our social community. We were hurt by the bigotry that is present in so many of our religious communities.

Yet, our children, as we knew them, did not fit the image of the ugly myths we had grown up with. Our daughters and sons were not weird people. They didn't look peculiar. They weren't molesting children. They weren't harming society in any way. They were solid citizens who were making valuable contributions to society with dignity and courage.

We have heard a story about people who spent their lives chained in a dark cave. The prisoners saw the reality of the outside world through shadows on the cave wall. Their concept of the world was a gross distortion, but it was the only truth they had. When we found out that our children were gay, we were like those prisoners in the cave. Our homophobia created our prison, and our beliefs, the old myths, were like the shadows on the wall. They were all we had to make some kind of sense of our situation. Replacing these myths with proven facts helped set us free. The facts gave us a base from which we could move into the light of reality.

It wasn't easy to unlearn old myths. We were confused, scared, and feeling guilty that we had failed as parents. Perhaps somebody knew something that we didn't know. Perhaps we had misjudged our children and were seeing them only through rose-colored glasses.

Floundering, many of us did what we had done frequently in the past. We tried to get a handle on things by looking for the origin, the cause. We asked ourselves, "What causes it? Did we cause it? Did somebody entice them into it and lead them astray?"

People who are further along in their acceptance tell us that we should not be concerned with cause; that we should be concerned with believing that being gay or lesbian is okay. And that it is a step many of us would eventually come to. But in the beginning, the cause of homosexuality filled our minds and could not be ignored.

There was another, more subtle reason that led us towards the search for cause. We hoped that a natural explanation for homosexuality could be found. We wanted to discover that gayness is a normal part of life, and therefore justifiable. What is natural is acceptable, whether we like it or not. Armed with such knowlege we would have something that could calm our damaging inner voices and lessen our confusion and guilt. Not having knowledge left us at the mercy of opinions.

Some lesbians and gays understandably resent it when parents are concerned about cause—especially if they don't understand that grieving parents first need to get out from under blame. The patience of gay children towards their parents' concern about cause is often rewarded. Parental anxiety about cause brings the first real confrontation with the shadows of old myths and usually acts as a spur to learning more about homosexuality.

After I'd go to bed at night, I'd mull things over in my mind. "Have I really been that dominant a mother? Curt made many of the decisions. He had his thumb on everything. We also made many decisions together, and even though I am more outspoken, that doesn't mean I'm dominant. I know Curt didn't play ball with the boys, but he was always around and available for the other youngsters and was interested in everything they did." I didn't see why this was happening to us, because we had done a lot "right." At least to us it felt right.

I worried a lot about why. Society has always said if your child does not measure up to the norm, it is the mother's fault. I am divorced, and I kept wondering if that had anything to do with Jay's being gay. For awhile, I even thought that one of "those" gays had done something to my son to entice him into a terrible life.

I was always much closer to Brian than my husband was. Brian and I often used to sit around and talk. I thought, "Was that unhealthy?" I looked back at all of our family life to see what was wrong in it. I figured there had to be something bad to cause this. At that time the only information I had was that homosexuality was caused by some sort of problem in the family.

The first thing you want to know is "Did I cause it?" We're taught that it's shameful and perverted to be gay, and when it happens to you, in your family, the guilt comes out immediately. So the first thing you're interested in is how much of it is your fault. I worried that I had hurt my daughter.

Since 1948 there have been only two comprehensive long-range studies that give hard facts about homosexuality. The earlier one was the famous Kinsey study published in two volumes in 1948 and 1952, entitled *Sexual Behavior in the Human Male* and *Sexual Behavior in the Human Female*. The more recent one was the Bell, Weinberg, and Hammersmith study published in 1982, *Sexual Preference: Its Development in Men and Women*. Both of these studies were conducted under the auspices of the Alfred C. Kinsey Institute for Sex Research at the University of Indiana at Bloomington, Indiana. Both meet the criteria of carefully designed research. Consequently, we relied on these two studies extensively.

We will examine twelve of the most commonly held myths, beginning with the ones that are the most difficult for parents—the myths concerning cause. Though there are numerous myths about cause, we chose four of the most common to report on. The cause myths are followed by a personal statement about cause which is based on our research and experience.

MYTH #1—NEUROTIC FAMILY PATTERNS CAUSE HOMOSEXUALITY

Most parents have suffered in one way or another from being told that a gay child is produced by a neurotic family. Such a family is described as being the combination of a dominant or seductive mother and a weak or distant father. There is a scientific ring to this falsehood which makes it difficult to ignore. We decided to find out the source of this myth.

Until the gay rights movement began in 1969, there was little research on homosexuality. The few studies that did exist tended to support the biases of the culture.

One work which was widely quoted was published in a book by Irving Bieber et al., *Homosexuality: A Psychoanalytic Study*.[1] It stated that male homosexuality is caused by an engulfing mother and/or a weak, distant, or hostile father.

Critics have pointed out that this study was characterized by the following poor research methods: only people who were in psychoanalysis were studied, no attempt was made to have a representative sample, there was no comparative control group, and the researchers made no attempt to eliminate researcher bias. As a result, the opinions presented in the study were just that—opinions, with no basis of fact to back them up. The study revealed more about psychoanalytic patients than about gays.[2]

Fortunately, the Alfred C. Kinsey Institute for Sex Research also decided to study the question of why some people are homosexual. The results of this work were published in the book, *Sexual Preference*, by Bell, Weinberg, and Hammersmith.[3]

These authors used careful methods in order to ensure that their conclusions would not be colored by old myths. Researchers Bell, Weinberg, and Hammersmith questioned 979 homosexuals and 477 heterosexuals who made up a representative and matched sample of the total population.[4] Their meticulous study took ten years to complete—three years in which to collect the data, five years to analyze it, and another two years to check it.[5] They found that family backgrounds had little or no effect on a person's eventual sexual orientation. One of the central passages in the book sums up a major finding that can help parents drop their guilt about cause.

> For the benefit of readers who are concerned about what parents may do to influence their children's sexual preference, we would restate our findings another way. No particular phenomenon of family life can be singled out, on the basis of our findings, as especially consequential for either homosexual or heterosexual development. You may supply your sons with footballs and your daughters with dolls, but no one can guarantee that they will enjoy them. *What we seem to have identified...is a pattern of feelings and reactions within the child that cannot be traced back to a single social or psychological root;* indeed, homosexuality may arise from a biological precursor (as do left-handedness and allergies, for example) that parents cannot control. In short, to concerned parents, we cannot recommend anything beyong the care, sympathy, and devotion that good parents presumably lavish on all their children anyway.[6]

The accurate studies tell us there are neurotic family patterns and there are loving family patterns. Both types of families produce heterosexual and homosexual children.[7]

MYTH #2—ACTING LIKE A SISSY OR TOMBOY CAUSES PEOPLE TO BE GAY

Some gay and lesbian children were at odds with their parents when they were growing up. A number of our parents reported that they were often left feeling frustrated and confused as they realized their child didn't follow the typical interest patterns of children their age; for example, a son who didn't enjoy competitive sports, such as baseball, or a daughter who did. Going outside of what our society considers typical— expected masculine or feminine behavior—is called by Bell, Weinberg, and Hammersmith "gender nonconformity."[8] It often left parents feeling like failures as they wondered, "Why isn't he or she like the other boys or girls? Did I fail to provide a good role model?" The following excerpts show the problem:

Matt, my gay son, didn't fit the mold, the macho male mold, that his brother, John, did. Matt didn't have any interest in sports. His interests were along a different line. He tried baseball, but it was hard for him because he was a little bit on the stout side. He was the last one to be put into the game, and he was the strike-out king. Oh, I was in Boy Scouts with him, but as he got older, it seemed we communicated less and less. There was a big wall between us.

One time when Matt was in high school, I sat him down and told him that I felt this wall; that I wanted to break it down but that it had to be a two-way street. I asked him to help me. He said he would, but we were never successful. And that wall was there until he told us he was gay.

I suffered a great deal of guilt about the way I had related to Alex when he was growing up. When he was a baby, things were fine, but as soon as he got to where he could go outside and play, I failed him miserably. I feel I didn't do enough with him. I tried to play with him as I did with Joe and Vickie, but he wouldn't go by the rules. He always tried to change them. He just wouldn't conform. I took him to things like Hi-Y and Cub Scouts and participated with him, but when it came to relating to each other every day, we just couldn't seem to hit it off.

By the time he was ten or twelve, he was very frustrated and dissatisfied. I think it was worse when he got old enough for competition. He could compete, but he didn't feel that he could. Sometime in there I think he put a name to his difference. He was very bright, and he read a lot.

I was frustrated because I didn't know what was wrong. I remember one time I told him I felt cheated because I never had the relationship with him that I wanted. I said, "You never let me do anything with you," which he didn't. He didn't fit the mold, my mold. I was probably terrified to bend enough to fit his mold, which is really terrible to say.

These fathers and their sons suffered from their inability to understand each other. Neither side had the necessary information to help break down the wall, even though they wanted to. Mothers, too, recalled being concerned about the "gender nonconformity" of their sons. Many of our interviewed parents had trouble admitting that their sons acted in any way feminine.

From a very early age I could see that Mike was what you might call more feminine than the masculine "ideal." We had to decide as parents how we were going to deal with that. He enjoyed a lot of things that girls typically like. It wasn't extreme, but he liked music, art, quiet games, and that sort of thing. He didn't go for rough play or for athletics in general.

I decided that I didn't want to make Mike self-conscious about his nature, but at the same time I did want to make "masculine" things available to him. So we went out of our way to teach him how to play ball. We did a lot of sports together as a family, which was fun because we all liked them. We went camping and did other rough-outdoor-activities. And from time to time we tried to interest him in things like Boy Scouts and Little League.

We would encourage him to take part in the usual "boy" activities, but we didn't want to make him feel uncomfortable if he didn't choose them. And he usually didn't choose them. He didn't like the rough-and-tumble. Although he did like camping and had some interest in certain sports, he didn't like contact sports. So we decided to keep off his back and let him do what appealed to him. Our goal was to make him comfortable with being whatever he was and not restrict him.

The nonconformity of a son tends to create more conflict than does such behavior in a daughter. Still, many parents reported that they noticed their daughter's lack of interest in traditionally "feminine" activities.

Thinking back over the years I remember there were several times when the possibility that Mary might be gay crossed my mind. But each time I brushed it from my mind and even felt guilty about having the thought.

Once when Mary was three years old she asked, "Do I always have to be a girl?" When she was growing up she liked the companionship of boys her age. She always enjoyed athletics even though she was not that good. She was never very interested in dolls. I can still picture her as a little girl with a softball in one hand, a bat in the other, and a toy gun in the holster on her hip.

When Melinda was little she was very much a tomboy, as I had been. I thought, "Well, she's a tomboy, but that's fine." She never did play with dolls. Neither did I. I had one doll in my whole life, and I hated it. I believed she was just behaving like I did.

I wondered if Melinda was gay when she was in high school, because her best friend was a tough-looking girl, and I didn't like that. I even asked Melinda if her friend was gay, but I never did ask Melinda if she was.

Even though we have many examples of parents who noticed nonconformity in their child, we also have examples from those who did not.

Jerry dated a little in high school. As I think back over it, there wasn't too much about his relationship with girls that would have led me to believe he was gay. He was a very good dancer, had a good personality and, if I say so myself, was very good-looking. Girls were always around here clamoring over him.

I was never so surprised in my life as when Cathy told me she was a lesbian. She was just what you would expect a little girl to be. She played with dolls and had crushes on boys. She even dated a lot in high school. She chose to wear dresses and was very feminine.

My son was "all boy" the whole time he was growing up. He liked sports and fishing. He was a good pitcher in Little League.

Usually, parents felt there was some lack in themselves that created the feminine actions of their sons or the masculine actions of their daughters, although parents were not as concerned about this kind of behavior on the part of the girls. They believed that such actions by boys indicated an unhappy and maladjusted child. They were also afraid that their sons would be subject to ridicule from classmates. As a result, some parents pressured their young children to change their natural behavior.

The authors of *Sexual Preference* believe that gender nonconformity may signal homosexuality for many gays and lesbians.

But it is not a cause. Of course, it would have been better if we parents had known that we had little to do with the gender nonconformity of our children. Unfortunately for everyone concerned, we did not.

We hope that this information will clear away some of the guilt that parents and children often feel when they look back over some of the parent-child conflicts of the early years together. As one father said so well, "Now I see that the problem in our relationship wasn't my fault, and it wasn't his. We were just caught up in something we couldn't understand."

MYTH #3—HOMOSEXUAL SEDUCTION CAUSES CHILDREN TO BE GAY

No other lie causes as much damage to our gay and lesbian children as does this one. People mount political hate campaigns in the name of saving the children. These campaigns have led to the denial of the basic democratic rights for gay and lesbian persons. Teachers lose their jobs if they are gay, even though there is absolutely no evidence that their being openly gay or otherwise will have any impact on their students' sexuality.

As with many of the ideas about cause, the authors of *Sexual Preference* found that neither gays nor lesbians were seduced into the homosexual life style.[9] There was a significant period of time between becoming aware of being gay or lesbian and acting on that awareness.[10] In fact, lesbian and gay adolescents often think they are alone. It is a frightening and sad time for them and can sometimes lead to tragic consequences.

MYTH #4—A TRAUMATIC EVENT WITH A PERSON OF THE OPPOSITE SEX CAN CAUSE HOMOSEXUALITY

There was no evidence to support this idea in the study done by Bell, Weinberg, and Hammersmith. Traumatic events caused pain for both gay and nongay people. But it did not cause them to change their sexual orientation.[11] Being gay or lesbian does not mean being angry with people of the opposite sex. It simply means being sexually attracted to people of the same sex.

A PERSONAL NOTE FROM THE AUTHORS ABOUT CAUSE

Each time a new research theory comes out about cause, parents tend to look inside themselves, as well as at their total family life. They often say to themselves, "Did I do that? Was our family like that? Maybe someone has found out something that will indict me! Maybe I am guilty of a crime against my son or daughter!" After awhile—when they are able to discriminate between fact and opinion—parents learn to reject the damage caused by their own negative thoughts and by the false opinions of others.

We wish we could say without question what the cause of homosexuality is. But as of this writing the cause is unknown. The scientific study of sexuality is in its infancy. Even the tools we use to investigate and measure with are primitive. The only statement we can make without hesitation is that parents should harbor no fears or guilt feelings that something in their parenting caused their child's homosexuality. These negative feelings can, and should, be dropped.

Before we go on with other myths that are not concerned with cause, we should explain our bias about this question. We lean toward a biological cause for two reasons. First, the latest and best research points that way. Second, it fits our experience.

We also want to see an end to the blame game that raises its ugly head with alarming regularity. When energy is spent on establishing blame, little is done to resolve issues. But, more than this, we believe that our society will accept gayness only if the vast majority of its citizens see it as a naturally occurring event. If most people understand that a certain percentage of society will be gay no matter what their family background is, or what their sexual experiences were, then gay people have a better chance of living their lives free from fears of retaliation.

There would be no need for books like this one. Parents could accept their children's gay life style as easily as they now accept left-handedness.

MYTH #5—GAY AND LESBIAN PEOPLE ARE MENTALLY SICK

In the face of overwhelming odds and much adversity, the majority of gays and lesbians are psychologically healthy. They are remarkably similar to their heterosexual counterparts. A minority of both groups are disturbed; a majority of both groups show good mental health. The percentages are the same.[12]

In a landmark study in 1957, Evelyn Hooker found that there was no significant difference in the mental health of homosexuals and heterosexuals.[13] This finding was confirmed by other studies. As a result, both the American Psychological Association and the American Psychiatric Association no longer list homosexuality as a mental illness.

Another study compared lesbian women to heterosexual women. Mark Freedman reported his work in the article, "Stimulus-Response: Homosexuals May Be Healthier Than Straights."[14] He found that lesbian women often functioned better than nongay women. They tended to be more candid and less defensive. They have a high degree of adaptability and often report a sense of freedom.

The following quote by John C. Gonsiorek was made after he had studied all the available research relating to homosexuality and mental illness:

> It is my contention that the issue of whether homosexuality per se is a sign of psychopathology, psychological maladjustment, or disturbance has been answered, and the answer is that it is not....This is not to say that psychologically disturbed homosexuals do not exist; nor does it mean that no homosexuals are disturbed because of their sexuality. Rather, the conclusion is that homosexuality in and of itself bears no necessary relationship to psychological adjustment. This should not be surprising; heterosexuals disturbed because of their sexuality fill many therapists' caseloads.[15]

MYTH #6—PEOPLE ARE EITHER HETEROSEXUAL OR HOMOSEXUAL

A commonly held myth is that people can be categorized as either homosexual or heterosexual. There is no in-between. But like so many other myths, this one is not supported by careful investigation.

In the famous Kinsey studies of the late 1940s and early 1950s, the researchers at the Institute for Sexual Research found that while many people classified themselves as exclusively heterosexual or exclusively homosexual, a large group had feelings and/or sexual experiences with people of both sexes. As a result, a new category was identified. Those who are attracted to members of both sexes were classified as bisexual. In the book, *Sexual Behavior in the Human Female* by the staff of the Institute for Sexual Research, Indiana University, the researchers developed a continuum for looking at sexual behavior which we shall reproduce here. This continuum in no way indicates the percentages of people in the categories. Rather, it simply illustrates the types of sexual orientations that exist in the population. Each and every person will fit somewhere on this continuum.

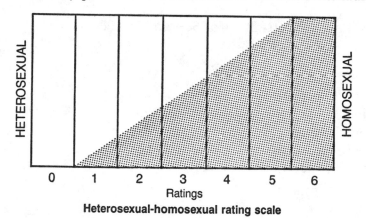

Heterosexual-homosexual rating scale

Definitions of the ratings are as follows: 0 = entirely heterosexual. 1 = largely heterosexual, but with incidental homosexual history. 2 = largely heterosexual, but with a distinct homosexual history. 3 = equally heterosexual and homosexual. 4 = largely homosexual, but with distinct heterosexual history. 5 = largely homosexual, but with incidental heterosexual history. 6 = entirely homosexual.

Adapted from *Sexual Behavior in the Human Female*[16]. Used by permission.

MYTH #7—GAYS AND LESBIANS ARE
FEW AND FAR BETWEEN

When we first started this book we thought it would be a simple matter to determine just how many people are gay and lesbian. But as we researched the available facts, we found that there was a vaguenss about the exact percentages. We read in several sources that ten percent of the population is predominately or exclusively gay or lesbian (numbers five and six on the Kinsey continuum). Other sources gave a figure of five percent.

However, calculations based on either of these percentages indicate that the number of gay people in our country is enormous. The following charts give the estimated number of homosexuals in the United States, as well as the numbers of parents affected because of the gayness of their children.

ESTIMATED POPULATION OF ALL GAY PEOPLE
AND THEIR PARENTS IN THE U.S.

Population of U.S., as of September 1984
236,000,000 (rounded)

	10%	5%
Number of gay people	23,600,000	11,800,000
Number of parents of gays and lesbians	47,200,000	23,600,000
Total number of gay and lesbian people and their parents	70,800,000	35,400,000

ESTIMATED POPULATION OF GAY PEOPLE OVER EIGHTEEN AND THEIR PARENTS IN THE U.S.

Population of U.S. over the age of 18,
as of September 1984
157,100,000 (rounded)

	10%	5%
Number of gay people	15,710,000	7,855,000
Number of parents of gays and lesbians	31,420,000	14,910,000
Total number of gay and lesbian people and their parents	47,130,000	22,765,000

Making the Figures Come to Life

The figures in both these charts for the estimated gay population are so great that they are mind boggling. We have trouble getting a personal picture of just what they mean. However, if we take each category separately, we can translate these statistics into a number that comes to life.

1. *The Ten Percent Category.* This category says that one out of every ten persons that you know is either predominantly or exclusively gay or lesbian. Of course, two more persons are affected because they are the parents of a gay or lesbian individual. On the average, a classroom full of children will have one in ten who is destined to be gay. Two out of ten parents at any school will have a gay or lesbian child. Adding up this category, three out of ten persons now suffer, directly or indirectly, from the homophobic fears of society.

2. *The Five Percent Category.* This more conservative estimate states that one in twenty will be primarily gay or lesbian. Two more in twenty will be parents of gays and lesbians.

Both of these categories show us that lesbians and gays are everywhere. They tell us that their parents are everywhere. All are subject in one way or another to the cruel prejudices of society. As one woman said, "When you attack homosexuality or make fun of gays and lesbians or think homosexual people should be denied their rights, you are sure to hurt someone you know and love. You're hurting a friend, a neighbor, a cousin, a niece, a nephew, a brother, a sister, a son, a daughter."

MYTH #8—GAYS AND LESBIANS CHOSE IT AND THEREFORE THEY CAN CHANGE IT

Choice and change are closely interrelated in the public mind. The belief goes: "If gay persons choose to be gay, then they can choose to not be gay. They can change. They do not have to act on their gay feelings. Therefore, all the forces of the society should be brought to bear on gay and lesbian persons to force them into the straight and narrow path of hetero-sexuality."

On the other hand, if gayness is a natural condition and is essentially impervious to change, then all of the efforts to change sexual orientation are a waste of time and effort. All the rhetoric which condemns gayness is then erroneous thinking. The denial of rights, the cruel jokes, the physical attacks against lesbians and gays are all signs of a society that needs to reexamine its values on this whole issue.

Parents, too, have a major stake in the choice/change controversy. Thinking that their child has a choice brings out instinctual fears. Many will not stop pressuring their child to conform. The choice/change mind-set also keeps parents from examining their old dreams, from taking the steps necessary to rearrange those dreams, and from accepting their child's right to be different.

Most modern therapists agree that a predominantly gay orientation cannot and should not be changed. Forcing a gay child to "shape up or ship out," no matter how lovingly done, is not an answer.

Most current research supports favors the belief that behaviors can be chosen, but basic orientation cannot. A person could choose not to act on gayness and to live a celibate life. And some gay people do so, preferring celibacy to the risk of rejection. They can also suppress their homosexuality, deny it, hate themselves for it. They may even choose to live a semblance of a heterosexual life. Experience seems to indicate that this is a recipe for unfulfillment at best, disaster at worst. The obvious conclusion drawn from this controversy is that the whole subject of our heterosexual or homosexual nature is, as yet, incompletely understood.

Once parents examine and discard the choice/change idea, their difficulty in accepting the gayness of their child is greatly eased. The uproar dies down, and everyone finds relief from the sense of danger that accompanies the issue of choice. They begin to see that homosexuality is normal—a bit unusual when viewed from their heterosexual orientation—but basically normal.

MYTH #9—GAYS AND LESBIANS ARE EASY TO IDENTIFY

The vast majority of lesbian and gay people are very much hidden. Howard Brown's book, *Familiar Faces, Hidden Lives*, sums up how most gay and lesbian people live. They are held back by fears of job loss, rejection by families, and a real sense of physical danger.

Some gays and lesbians do choose to let the nongay world know what their sexual orientation is. Out of this group, a very small number reveal their gayness with behavior or dress that fits the commonly held stereotype. These actions say to the world, "I am me. I will not deny my sexual nature. I will handle whatever I have to face."

There is another group of gay people who are easy to identify—those who freely get into the fight for gay rights and come out in all phases of their lives. The benefits they have won for all gay people far outweigh their small number. They have made life easier for everyone associated with the gay community. By refusing to disappear, these activists are forcing society to acknowledge them. They do not accept the oppressive tactics that are being used against them and their brothers and sisters.

Many other gay people choose to be identified in a limited way. They come out to particular groups such as their family or friends or fellow workers. Even this partial coming out challenges the stereotype and lessens society's attack on the homosexual life style. Only the most insensitive people can ridicule or condemn a relative or a good friend or a person they work with every day.

Most of us have been guilty of thinking we can identify gays and lesbians from their outward appearance or behavior. Because we knew some, we assumed we could recognize all. The truth is if all gay people decided to wear a purple hat on a given day, we would be amazed at their numbers. Letha Scanzoni punctures the smugness of many of us in a recent article:

> One lesbian told me, "It kills me that people sit around talking stereotypically about gays and don't know they're sitting next to one in church."

> Similarly, another woman told of a time when a professional colleague pointed out a stranger on the street and said, "That man is a homosexual. I can spot one anytime, just by looking at them." She recalled thinking, "Oh, if you could only know! You've worked with me for nearly a quarter of a century—and have never guessed my orientation. And because of your anxiety and hostility over this topic, I'll never be able to share this part of myself with you, even though you think of me as your friend."

> In another case, a pastor boasted of his ability to detect homosexual persons because "the Holy Spirit bore witness" in his heart whenever a gay person happened on the scene. Yet he hadn't the foggiest notion that his highly esteemed assistant pastor, living celibately, had struggled for years to come to terms with his own homosexual orientation.[17]

MYTH #10—GAY AND LESBIAN PERSONS ARE POOR PARENTS SINCE THEY DO NOT CARE FOR FAMILY LIFE

Most gay people spend a great deal of their early lives trying desperately to fit into the heterosexual version of family life or grieving over their inability to do so. Some marry in the hope that they will somehow not be who they are. Others never tell their parents of their sexual orientation because they fear rejection. They do not want to lose their connection with their childhood nuclear family.

Many gay people, both men and women, express a deep longing for a family of their own. They want a long-term, loving, stable relationship, as well as children. Some do have children, either from a previous marriage or by artificial insemination or adoption. These children seem to grow up and adjust well; however, research on this subject is slim. Gay parents are reluctant to participate in studies because it is so easy for them to lose custody.

As a result, we could find no studies that have been done on the children who are raised by gay fathers. However, there was one anecdotal book, *Whose Child Cries* by Joe Gantz, that featured interviews with these children.[18] While the children were concerned about having to hide their parents' orientation, there was no basic psychological damage. Also, they were well taken care of physically and were fitting comfortably into society.

We did find that a small number of scientific studies had been done on lesbian mothers. Again there was no higher incidence of emotional disturbance, and the children did not have sexual identity problems.[19] In short, gay and lesbian people have family values and goals similar to those of nongay people.

MYTH #11—ALL GAY AND LESBIAN PEOPLE ARE OVERSEXED, AND INDISCRIMINATELY PROMISCUOUS

Before I found out about my gay son, I had this ridiculous belief that a gay or lesbian would try to get any person, heterosexual or homosexual, to have sex with them. I'm ashamed now that I thought that.

This parent has since found out that gay people have little or no sexual interest in heterosexuals or in indiscriminate sex. Sexuality is not the only focus of their lives any more than it is for heterosexuals.

While promiscuity does exist in the gay community, it is not nearly as extensive as we have been led to believe. There is as much diversity in sexual patterns in the gay community as there is in the heterosexual community. In fact, gay men are much more like nongay men in their sexual activity than they are like lesbian women. Conversely, lesbian women are more like nongay women in their sexual activity than like gay men.

It is quite possible that the promiscuity exhibited by some gay men may be due to the way society treats them. Gay people live in a McCarthy-like atmosphere, filled with a sense of danger and insecurity. They are often fearful of losing their jobs. They can be forced to move out of their homes. They can be expelled from the armed services. They can be denied security clearance. When faced with the tragedy of AIDS (Acquired Immune Deficiency Syndrome), they are told by some religious groups that they are receiving punishment from God. Their monogamous relationships are not honored legally or socially. Living under this barrage of attacks, some gay people may act in self-destructive ways.

But we have talked to other gay men who have given us a different perspective. They do not see promiscuity in black and white terms. They say for many gays it is a means of exploration and adventure; a way of giving and getting affection.

The idea of promiscuity is clearly one that troubles most parents. But care should be taken that a double standard not be used to judge our gay children. Promiscuity and extra-marital affairs are very much present in the heterosexual world.

I have been thinking about my gay son's sexuality. It was hard to even let it into my mind. It's really none of my business what he does in bed. I don't see sex in the same way my children do. I can't even understand all the ideas my straight children have about sex, much less my gay son's. I've decided to live and let live. Of course I can't help but worry about his health.

MYTH #12—GAYS AND LESBIANS LIVE A LONELY LIFE AND CONTRIBUTE NOTHING TO SOCIETY

The generalized homophobic picture of gay and lesbian life is that loneliness is pervasive. In truth, gay men and lesbian women live very much like their nongay counterparts. Many establish long-term monogamous relationships out of the desire to spend their lives with one person. David P. McWhirter and Andrew M. Mattison in their book, *The Male Couple,* have investigated the lives of long-term male couples. They found that gay men go through stages in their lives together, as the problems of learning to adjust to each other are worked out. These stages are similar to the stages of heterosexual marriage.

Overall, the gay and lesbian community provides a haven for its members. There is love and fun and support. There is self-acceptance and understanding. There is hope and commitment. All these are qualities that any good community would take pride in.

We asked a young gay man to talk about the specific ways that the gay culture supports its members and enhances the rest of society. Here are some highlights from his response. His pride and awareness of his own worth are shared by many gays and lesbians.

I think there are some special features in gay community life, but I wouldn't want people to assume that all gay people have to fit them. We have to be careful about generalizations. Although they can contain important truths, they can also limit the vision of who gay people are.

There is a lot of humor among gay people. There is a sense of playfulness and revelry. You can see some of it in the gay pride parades when people dress up in colorful and humorous costumes. And it's there in daily life too. There's a whole satirical tradition called camp that includes a secret language that people on the inside can appreciate. Words like "butch, dyke, queen, sissy, fairy, queer" which in the straight world are used in a derogatory way, may be used by gay people in a humorous, appreciative way.

Then there is also a serious side in the gay style, a sense of the tragic aspects of life, which is very deep and rich among gay and lesbian people. Part of this is because of the suffering in our homophobic society, but also I think gays and lesbians are more sensitive. I know that's the stereotype, but I think it is true that as a group, we are more tuned into emotional life, spiritual life, close communication, how people feel, and the price that is paid for ignoring these feelings.

In terms of contributions to the broader culture, I think that the arts and the nurturing professions are two expressions of this greater sensitivity. A lot of great writers, performers, and artists have been gay, partly because we have a very pronounced sense of the sorrow of life. As a group, there is a great depth of understanding. If you could remove all of the books, plays, and movies by gays, the gay actors, dancers, clowns, animal trainers, nurses, teachers, social workers, psychologists, therapists, you'd see a lot of blank spaces in American artistic and work life.

There is a strong sense of solidarity in both the gay and lesbian communities. We do an incredible amount of taking care of each other. If straight people could open their eyes to this, it could be an example for them.

We have always been active in social and political movements. Someone could write a book documenting the participation of gay people in the civil rights movement, the anti-war movement, the farm worker movement, the anti-imperialist movement. We participate out of proportion to our numbers.

In various and sundry ways, we nudge the society along. I think that's partly because many of us are not as bound by large families. We can afford to be catalysts for change. We have more freedom to be innovators. Because gay people have often been excluded from mainstream American life, they have had to live by their wits, create their own resources, and develop the courage to be their own persons.

THE DAMAGE OF SWEEPING GENERALIZATIONS

The injustice our children have to face because of these myths is extensive. Naturally healthy gays and lesbians are treated as though they have an incurable basic flaw and should be quarantined. Because of this attitude, they are exploited by unethical political and religious leaders who stand to gain from the devaluation and disenfranchisement of gay people. By pandering to the inner fears of the general population, these people gain power and financial advantage while using our children as scapegoats.

The facts we gained so far have been important for a sane perspective. But our education was also furthered by personal interaction with a variety of people.

NOTES FOR CHAPTER 2

[1]Irving Bieber et al., eds., *Homosexuality: A Psychoanalytic Study* (New York: Basic Books, 1962).

[2]For an analysis and critique see two studies: a) William Paul et al., eds., *Homosexuality: Social, Psychological and Biological Issues* (Beverly Hills, CA: Sage Publications, Inc., 1982) pp. 68-69, 81-82, 128-129, and b) Noretta Koertge, ed., *Nature and Causes of Homosexuality: A Philosophic and Scientific Inquiry* (New York: The Haworth Press, 1982) p. 61.

[3]Alan P. Bell, Martin S. Weinberg, and Sue K. Hammersmith, *Sexual Preference: Its Development in Men and Women* (Bloomington: Indiana University Press, 1981).

[4]Ibid. p. 9.

[5]Ibid. p. 238. (The breakdown of the number of years spent in the study was provided in a lecture by Martin Weinberg.)

[6]Ibid. pp. 191-192. (Italics in text.)

[7]Ibid. pp. 183-184.

[8]Ibid. p. 188

[9]Ibid. p. 185.

[10]Ibid. pp. 187-188.

[11]Ibid. p. 185.

[12]William Paul et al., eds., "Results of Psychological Testing on Homosexual Populations," pp. 73-74, *Homosexuality: Social, Psychological and Biological Issues.* Copyright © 1982 by Sage Publications, Inc., Beverly Hills. Reprinted by permission of Sage Publications, Inc.

[13]Evelyn A. Hooker, "The Adjustment of the Male Overt Homosexual," *Journal of Protective Techniques*, 21 no. 1 (1957) 17-31.

[14]Mark Freedman, "Stimulus-Response: Homosexuals May Be Healthier Than Straights," *Psychology Today*, 8, no. 10 (March 1975) 28-32.

[15]Paul, op. cit. pp. 78-79.

[16]Alfred C. Kinsey et al., *Sexual Behavior in the Human Female* (Philadelphia: W.B. Saunders Co., 1953) p. 470.

[17]Letha Dawson Scanzoni, "Putting a Face on Homosexuality," *The Other Side*, Issue 149 (February 1984) p. 8. Reprinted with permission from *The Other Side* magazine, 300 W. Apsley Street, Philadelphia, PA 19144.

[18]Joe Gantz, *Whose Child Cries: Children of Gay Parents Talk About Their Lives* (Rolling Hills Estates, CA: Jalmar Press, 1983).

[19]Paul, op. cit. p. 280.

chapter *3*

Communicating with Others

Healing can happen if you receive two things: knowledge and human support.

The best available tool is the "grief cycle," but for most people the cycle will not be complete unless they share their grief with someone who has been through a similar experience.[1]

Books by careful researchers and by people honestly knowledgeable about homosexuality can help parents in many important ways. But reading was not enough for most of us. We had to talk out our grief and fears.

Honest talk was the key ingredient. Healing accelerated as we shared our feelings with people who were willing to listen, willing to understand the hurt, and willing to tell of their own feelings. This help came from a variety of sources—a good friend, our own gay child, other parents of gays and lesbians, other gays and lesbians, and/or the right type of counselor.

TELLING A FRIEND

Sharing our hurt with a close friend can be a great source of comfort.

I called my best friend and told her. She said, "What do you want me to say to you?" I answered that I wanted her to tell me she loved me and that everything was going to be okay. At that time I needed to have a sense of belonging to someone. I needed to feel that I was not a failure, that I had tried.

And she said, "Of course I love you. Don's sexuality has nothing to do with our relationship." She really pulled it together for me. She understood what I was going through.

GETTING HELP FROM OUR OWN CHILD

Some of us found another source of help—a source even closer to home—our own gay son or lesbian daughter. Many parents gratefully told of the help they received from their children.

I didn't know much when I first found out. So I started coming up with all these questions for my son. I was fortunate because Don would always answer them. Sometimes he didn't like the questions and would laugh at them, but he always gave me truthful answers no matter how silly he thought they were. That helped me a great deal.

I remember once I even asked him if he hung around in the restrooms at the park. He said, "Only when I have to urinate." That was the answer I needed. I had so many bad thoughts because of what I was reading in the paper. Talking to Don and finding out how he felt took away these scary ideas. He gave me books, too. I wanted to know. It was important for me to know.

I think my relationship with Robin is closer now. Before there was always this barrier. Now I know precisely where I stand. Our relationship is open, and we can talk about everything.

We always did have a good relationship when she was growing up. But it took me time before I could talk about her lesbianism without getting hysterical. Then there was a period when I never brought it up to her, and she never brought it up to me. Now I can even joke with her and tease her a little bit. I think that's a real sign that I have accepted it.

I made some efforts to talk more with Jerry. I was pretty pointed in the things I asked him, because I really didn't know much about homosexuality.

Anytime Jerry came home he would explain his feelings, and then my husband and I could see it a little more clearly through his eyes. Sometimes we would write him. We would even call him on the phone. He was the one who had the experience. We did not. We were the fledglings, the learners. He was the teacher.

Finally, after several months, I said to my son, "There have been many things on my mind, and one of the things I'm wondering is how can I be supportive in this? What do you want me to do?" And he said, "Nothing special—just whatever you feel is right. If you're uncomfortable about anything, ask me any questions. Talk to me about whatever is bothering you."

One of my initial reactions was "He's going to be so badly hurt when he's rejected." But he hasn't been. He was totally prepared for the fact that certain people who were his friends suddenly aren't anymore. He doesn't care. He feels that it's their problem, not his.

Some of his healthy attitude rubbed off on me, because I had been so afraid of other people's opinions. Now I find I no longer care what people think.

LEARNING FROM OTHER GAYS AND LESBIANS

There is another dimension that plays a critical role: meeting and getting to know other lesbians and gay men. In the beginning, the only gay or lesbian that we *know* we know is our own child. We are afraid that if we meet other homosexuals then we'll discover that all those scary stories we've heard are true. It takes time to realize that having access to gay people in natural situations is a vital resource for getting in touch with the truths about gayness. We found that our fears were unfounded.

All the information you can get, plus support from other parents, isn't enough to convince you at a deeper level that lesbians and gays are

*okay as people. It isn't until you meet gay people, and share with them
something about your lives that big changes begin to occur.*

*Without meeting gay people you can't really shake the homo-
phobia. When we talk together in our rap groups, we share a common
pain, sometimes including tears. Then a bond gradually builds. The
stereotypes just fall away. It doesn't matter that Joan is lesbian and Bill
is gay. As we grow together, our fondness for one another grows. We
become willing to stand up for each other against the hurts of a hostile
world.*

―――――――――――

*At one Parents FLAG meeting I was talking to a young lesbian,
and I said, "Just think of all the hurt my daughter is going to go
through." She said, "But that's your definition of what hurt is. That may
not be the way your daughter or I would react." That helped ease some of
my fears.*

LEARNING FROM COUNSELORS

Some of us found help from counselors. It is important,
however, that parents be careful in their selection of a counselor or therapist because many of them are not up-to-date
about homosexuality.

Even though the American Psychiatric Association has
removed homosexuality from its list of mental disorders, and
the American Psychological Association and the American
Nurses Association have called for an end to discrimination
against homosexuality, we are still in a period of transition.
Too many therapists hang onto the "desirability" of heterosexuality. Such professionals do damage to gay men, lesbians, and
their parents. We urge those parents who seek professional
help to ask what the therapist believes about gayness. Do not go
to someone who is negative or who views homosexuality as
something that should or could be changed.

*First, I went to a counselor at our group health center. She was a
warm, motherly person, and with a gentle smile, she told me, "I think it's
just a phase. He is probably in a rebellious stage, trying to get your*

*attention. Keep contact with him, and he'll probably grow out of it."
That's just what I wanted to hear; but as I look back on it, I see that
although she had good intentions, she was really as ignorant on the
subject as I was. Her training had taught her that being gay was
misbehavior or arrested development.*

*Later I joined a therapy group with a counselor who had a very
different attitude. One of her first questions was "Are you and Jack
blaming each other?" I said we weren't. I had a lot of confused thoughts
at the time. She assured me that we need not get into blaming someone;
that homosexuality was just part of the human condition. Chris could
live a happy, productive life. Our job was to learn to live with it in non-
destructive ways.*

---

*I started looking for a counselor who knew the facts about
homosexuality and could make me feel better. After the exhilaration of
finally meeting with one, I experienced some depression. I began to
realize that although my "head trip" had been very effective and intense,
I had not really dealt with the grief. Through continued help from a
skilled counselor, I worked through much grief.*

There are both gay and nongay therapists who have well-
grounded knowledge about homosexuality, and who can help
parents become clearly informed about the subject. With these
therapists, parents can get valuable help in dealing with their
feelings and clarifying their attitudes.

*I was in a counseling group when Barbara told us, and that was a
big help. I had been fighting depression, with terrible feelings about
being a failure as a teacher. I felt I might not be able to go on. When I
got the news about Barbara, it just felt like the last straw.*

*Fortunately for me, the therapist and group members were
nonjudgmental about gayness. I got support when I needed it.*

*It took me some years to work through different phases to the point
where I now feel good about Barbara and myself, and I can go out and
work for gay rights. But the group therapy at that early time helped me
through one of the hardest times. I was lucky.*

RECEIVING SUPPORT FROM OTHER
PARENTS OF GAY PEOPLE

Over and over again, we heard parents say that finding the way to other parents of gay people or to a parent support group became an important turning point. It is much easier to move away from an awful sense of loneliness if we share it with someone who has experienced the same thing. It's a relief to discover that these other parents are so much like ourselves— they share the common goal of learning to understand themselves and their children.

I was sick and a special friend came to see me, bringing with her—believe it or not—some of her homemade chicken soup. My pain about Linda was so great I could not hide it any longer. The hour that followed was filled with tears and anguish. When I finished she said quietly, "I think I understand. That is our situation, too. Our son is gay. I know how it feels, but if it is any comfort to you, it won't seem so painful two years from now."

At last I had someone with whom I could share. And what a difference! That was the first step towards healing. Also the first step towards entering into the nameless world where probably one in ten human beings suffers as a result of being so little understood and so maligned.

I had read about a parents of gays' group in an Ann Landers column. I wrote a letter to the post office box listed in the column. It was the hardest thing I've ever done in my life. For all I knew, the parents' group was some kooky organization. I had all sorts of thoughts that maybe they would put our name in the papers or something like that. But I wrote that letter anyway, because we were desperate to talk to somebody. We were eager to meet other people who were willing to admit they had a homosexual child.

The other parents at the first meeting had been where we were. It was comforting to know that we were not going through this alone. It was the sense of a common bond—that they were all trying to accept it or tolerate it or cope with it—that was just comforting. It did something for us. We could face the world again. I wouldn't take anything for the people we've met in the group.

We felt we had no one, no one to talk to except each other, and we had exhausted the subject. When we finally got to the parents' group, it was so good to be with other people and exchange experiences and ideas and thoughts and the pain that you feel at first. And then we began to go through the different levels, towards acceptance.

I don't think I had been in that first meeting very long when I made a commitment to myself—that I would keep coming back. It was easy for me to see that this wasn't a place where people came to look and point at each other. Instead they came to try to help one another with their problems.

Andy was only seven when his father died, and he was the youngest child. I thought about how I brought him up after that, and I can't think how I could have done it any other way. I also took large doses of hormones before he was born, because I'd had a series of miscarriages previously. Yet, in the support group I'm the only one who had had these experiences. It proved to me that those things didn't cause the homosexuality. I'm forever grateful that there was a group to go to when I needed it. Parents need to know there is someone else with the same problems.

I have a great time at the parents' meeting. I've been thinking about that lately and decided that it is our sharing of the tough things that brings us closer. We can be ourselves, and we can talk about the part of ourselves that is vulnerable. We're having fun at the same time. The group has a purpose and there are nice people in it. When we are together, we can be who we are and not fear being condemned. I feel that I can say almost anything about myself in that group. It's comfortable.

The following interchange between Virginia and Fran occurred during an interview conducted for this book. We present it at some length because it reveals the mutual aid that can develop between parents of gay people who have built trust in each other.

Virginia: *Why don't you start out by telling how your son came out to you?*

Fran: *It was about five years ago when Ed wrote Hal and me a letter. Hal is my other son. Ed just wrote that he was gay. He said that he had felt from very early childhood that he was different. He had had sex with girls, but it was distasteful to him. He knew that it could never be any other way but homosexual for him.*

He told me that he had always felt conflict between us and that he hoped his telling me would clear it up. That feeling is all gone now. We both understand how and why there was a strain in our relationship.

I had always suspected, even from early childhood. His father was overseas until Ed was a year old. The first time he saw Ed he said, "He walks like a girl." Ed was always effeminate and got along better with girls as a young boy in grade school. He played with girls and was always teased by the boys. It wasn't until high school, when he got into drama, that he was able to relate to both sexes.

It was at this time that his father and I went through a divorce. I was going to move from California to the Midwest, and Ed begged me not to. (She cries.) I knew I wouldn't get through this.

Virginia: *It really does upset you a lot.*

Fran: *Ed begged me not to move because he said he just knew he couldn't get along here in the Midwest. So we did stay another year. He graduated, and he had good relationships with his peers for the first time in his life. Now he's in California where he has lots of friends.*

Virginia: *You still feel a sense of loss?*

Fran: *Very much so. (She cries.) Although we can't say why he is a homosexual, I believe he was born that way. I think true homosexuals are all born that way. Because of our religion, I always hope and pray that he will change. But I really don't expect it. You know, I'm very proud of the way he conducts himself. His homosexuality is just a very small part of him.*

Virginia: *It seemed to touch on something very deep when you started talking about this awhile ago.*

Fran: *Well, I know what he has to go through as a gay man. It's a hard life for him. I think he would be a good family man if he could marry and have children. He has even said that he hopes he can figure some way to have children. That's how much he wants a family. I would certainly like to have normal family relationships with grandchildren. This part of it is a real heartbreaker.*

Virginia: *Is that what bothers you the most? The lack of an accepted family situation?*

Fran: *That and the fact that he has to be in California. I miss him, but he can't live a normal life here. I would like for us all to be together like other families. But I can't be open with the rest of my family about his situation.*

Virginia: *It's pretty lonely.*

Fran: *Yes. It hurts not being able to communicate. I feel like I'm always leading a double life, always on guard. I guess I'm in the closet more than he is. The only place I can talk about him is in the parents' group. That group helps me more than anything else. Talking to the other parents proved to me that I wasn't weird because this has happened. It wasn't because of the bad marriage.*

Virginia: *It sounds as if you feel very uncomfortable about this double life you're describing.*

Fran: *I always do. I think the big hang-up is religion. I still worry about his acceptance in the church.*

Virginia: *It's hard for you to accept what the church says knowing how he has to live.*

Fran: *Right.*

Virginia: *You're deeply religious and you feel pulled both ways.*

Fran: *I was at one time. Now I'm beginning to wonder about the church and all its rules. I don't really feel like they've helped people on an individual basis. What happens to me doesn't seem to really matter. Am I making any sense?*

Virginia: *You're making a lot of sense. What would you like from the church?*

Fran: *Some understanding.* (She cries.) *I feel really persecuted in the church. I just think the priests don't really understand what people go through. If you try and give it your best shot and don't make it, you shouldn't be persecuted.*

Virginia: *So, you feel like there are a couple of areas where you have not made it—a gay son and a divorce?*

Fran: *I did the best I could in both areas. I know I did. I think I should be excused. You can only take so much. You can't do any more. You can't force people to fit into a mold. I'm going to try to be as happy as I can be; I want Ed to be as happy as he can be. But I can't make church members and family members see that.*

Virginia: *That sounds strong. Do you feel strong when you say that?*

Fran: *Right. But of course I couldn't make them understand because I've never really said it before.* (They laugh.)

Virginia: *Church doctrine changes, Fran. The doctrine of any church is only an interpretation of the Word. The doctrine changes as society changes.*

Fran: *It's kind of backward right now.*

Virginia: *There's a minority group of people in your religion who view being gay in a pretty good light. You can choose to believe the negative view or you can choose to believe the positive. I feel better when I look at my son's gayness in as positive a light as possible.*

Fran: *You seem to know just what I need. I always feel better when I talk with you and the other people in the group. It just doesn't stay with me long enough.*

Virginia: *It's no wonder. You're all by yourself.*

Fran: *I can't even talk with Hal about it. He doesn't agree with it either.*

Virginia: *It's not a matter of agreeing or disagreeing when you really get down to it, Fran. It's a matter of "he is or he is not." Ed is gay and can't be otherwise.*

Fran: *I know that in my head. Yet sometimes I find it difficult to be around Ed for very long. His ways are just different from what I'm used to. He's different from what you'd expect of a traditional male.*

Virginia: *Is he effeminate?*

Fran: *Yes. That kind of tears me up. It's hard for me to agree with that part of him.*

Virginia: *Would you want to change him?*

Fran: *He's always been rather uninhibited. He does little things that are unusual, like bleaching his hair and talking to the animals at the zoo. I watched him do that, and it embarrassed me. You don't see many people standing around talking to the animals.* (They laugh.)

But afterwards I felt guilty. I love him, and yet I'm bothered by some of his actions. I wouldn't want to change him. He is the way he is. If I could change him, he wouldn't be the same boy.

Virginia: *Have you ever thought about the fact that at the time you found out he was gay, you lost him in a special kind of way? It happened about the same time you lost the sense of security that went with being married. You also lost your husband. You really had a mass of losses, all at the same time.*

Fran: *That's what part of this feeling I have is all about. It took me a year to tell my parents that I was divorced. I didn't want them to worry.*

I never told my mother about Ed's being gay. I'm afraid that it would be devastating for her. She's 78, and I doubt she could accept it. I don't talk about it anywhere except at our group. I have to take another step if I'm going to talk about Ed to my family or in public.

Virginia: *It takes awhile, Fran. Don't push yourself too soon. Are you beginning to feel that it's time for you to take another step?*

Fran: *Yes, I think so. If I could do it without crying.*

Virginia: *Try to be whatever you are at the moment. Because what you are is a super person. If you feel like crying, then I don't think you've cried enough.*

Fran: *But it's been five years.* (Her voice breaks.)

Virginia: *Feeling okay didn't come easy for me. I had the same kind of struggle. It gets even lonelier if you think other people are doing better than you are. It has been hard for me too. There's nothing wrong with you because you're still struggling. I just want you to know you don't have to struggle alone. Call me whenever you feel upset.*

Fran: *I'd like to get to the place where I wouldn't be crying when I talk about Ed's being gay. I'd like to be able to talk about it like you do. I want to be open.*

Virginia: *It is nice. I was surprised at how much better I felt after I became more open. I had thought it was better to stay behind a wall. But it wasn't.*

Fran, you seem to be on a treadmill, and you've been on that treadmill for a long time. And you sound as if you're tired of it.

Fran: *Yes! I'm a pretty open person. I hate to have all these secrets. I want to be able to just say what I think and feel.*

In the back of my mind I keep Mother as a big excuse to hold myself in. Oh, I don't know if that is all it is, but we have always kept everything from my mother. If I hurt her in any way, I might not ever forgive myself.

But when Ed was here, he asked why I didn't tell everyone. I told him I just couldn't. It's really up to him whether he wants to tell them or not.

Virginia: *It's also partly up to you though, isn't it?*

Fran: *Yes, right. I guess my mother is more my responsibility than his. I worry about how she would accept it and what it would do to her.*

Virginia: *Can you really expect your family to accept Ed's being gay better than you have? They might not accept it at first, but later they may change—as you have.*

Fran: *My whole family has the same Christian background. I know they would have the same feelings I have had.*

Virginia: *I'm just saying that even if you tell somebody and they don't approve, you can understand where their feelings come from.*

Fran: *When you tell somebody, Virginia, what kind of atmosphere do you tell them in?*

Virginia: *As I have changed my own feelings, I have told about my son in different ways. At first I cried. I got the comfort that I needed. Later I was more matter-of-fact about it because I wanted to educate people to the fact that I had a gay son, and that I didn't want to hear any gay jokes. Whatever you're feeling at the time is the way you tell about it. At least it was for me.*

Fran: *It takes a lot to speak up. Right now I can only come out in the group because there aren't many Catholics there. And the ones who are there agree with me.*

If I spoke out in my own territory or my own family, I'd be clobbered. I'll probably just sit and be a quiet little mouse like I always have been.

Virginia: *Fran, there is inside of you a very articulate, a very capable, a very strong person who is having a hard time keeping quiet.*

Fran: *Thank you. I'm glad you got that on tape.* (She laughs.)

Virginia: *I'll tell you what—there is a question I'd like to ask you that I think might be interesting. I'll ask it and then you can answer or not. Knowing that homosexuality is probably biological for most gay people, would you have treated Ed any differently than you did?*

Fran: *No, I don't see how I could have. I always felt that what I did at the time was the best thing I could do.*

Virginia: *You thought it through?*

Fran: *Right.*

Virginia: *Didn't try to make him into something he wasn't?*

Fran: *No, I always tried to help him be himself. There were times when he was playing with the girls that I would, you know, try to get him to play with the boys. But he just didn't fit in. It wasn't until high school when the boys were switching to the girls that he was switching to the boys.* (They laugh.) *You can't change something that strong. For the same reason, when I discovered that he was left-handed I never tried to change him to using his right hand. I knew it just wouldn't be him.*

Virginia: *So early on you accepted him for what he was?*
Fran: *Right, yes. It's something that was just meant to be.*

It is clear from the talk between Virginia and Fran that religion can be one of the most disturbing concerns of parents of gays. We heard this concern expressed so often that we decided to investigate the religious issues more closely.

NOTE FOR CHAPTER 3

[1]Rev. Kenneth Czillinger, *Newsletter*, American Association of Retired People (March 1983).

chapter 4

Winds of Change in Religious Thinking

If we as Christians are going to minister to gay people in Christ's name, we first must stop viewing homosexual orientation and homosexual persons in the abstract. We must allow the subject to become personalized to us....As we stop keeping homosexuality at a distance, as an abstract, and as we see it up close, with a face, something happens to us. We begin to see we are dealing with real human beings made in God's image. And we begin to feel the pain of bearing a stigma and experiencing the oppression and fear as though it were happening to us.[1]

Some people don't want to understand. And there are many unqualified moral judges sitting in a lot of church pews. It has been a great comfort that Jesus said nothing about this issue. But he did say a lot about judging.

The minister quoted scripture and said that the homosexual life style is a perversion according to Christian biblical principles. "It is a very damaging way of life. Remember Corinthians: 'Do not be deceived; neither the immoral, nor idolators, nor homosexuals, nor thieves, nor the greedy, nor drunkards, nor revilers, nor robbers will inherit the kingdom of God.'" (I Corinthians 6:9)

Will homosexuals go to hell? There is no doubt that for a sizable number of parents that is a real and distressing question. For many of them anxiety about religion is the source of some of their most painful feelings. Questions about this issue need to be resolved if parents are to be at peace with their child's homosexuality.

The statements at the opening of this chapter are examples of the range of attitudes present in the religious communities. Many parents are under the spell of fundamentalist ideas such as those expressed by the minister in the third paragraph. But new attitudes are emerging that challenge the ancient rejections.

We begin with comments from our parents that show the fear and pain, confusion and anger that welled up in them as they compared the goodness of their gay child with the condemning attitudes.

When I first found out, I gave up every thought of religion. I wondered how God could possibly do this to Tim. He already had the handicap of deafness and had learned to cope with it. I would go to the basement, and I would cuss and denounce God. I felt just terrible. I had this horrible black cloud hanging over me. I would shake my fist and cry, "How can you do this to me? How can you do this to Tim? Why does he have to have this on top of his deafness?" Nobody could hear me because I was down in my basement. I really had a rough time.

When I finally discussed it with my other son, I told him, "I don't believe in God. God couldn't do that. I'll never go to church again. I'll never believe—never, never, never."

All the time I was hating God. One day I took one of my little religious statues and broke it. "I'll never have you in my house again. I'll never pray to you again." Paul would say, "Now, Mom, you know God didn't have anything to do with it."

I was in this horrible condition for about six weeks. Because I was afraid I'd start to cry, I didn't want to talk to anybody, didn't want anybody to come around or anything. Then things started to get better. But for awhile—because of our upbringing in a little country town—we sure were hurt. There's no question about that. Something like being gay was completely taboo in our town. I mean gays were outcasts. But now we know that they're outcasts in the big cities, too.

Pretty soon after Don came out to me, he was interviewed by a reporter from the paper. The article appeared—with a picture—on page two of the Sunday paper. It identified Don and a friend of his as professed homosexuals. There it was, the fact that my son was gay, before God and everybody.

All my kids have graduated from Catholic schools, and my youngest was in eighth grade at the time. It was important to me that my kids attend Catholic schools, but because I raised them alone, it was hard for me to get up the money. I had this deal with the priest that when I got my income tax check, I would pay the tuition.

But that year I received letters from the school saying I was delinquent. I called the priest and said, "Father, I keep getting these letters, and I want to know what is going on."

He hesitated, then finally said, "Maybe you'd better come up here and we'll talk about it." When I went over, Father sat there and stammered. The more he stammered, the redder he got. Finally he said, "Rumor has it that Don condones the homosexual way of life. I can remember that he used to be such a good boy. He used to come to mass every day."

And I said to him, "Father, that's no rumor. He is homosexual, and he's still a good boy. He still goes to mass every day. His sexuality has nothing to do with how good he is. I walked in here because it was important for my daughter to stay in this school. But if this is the kind of Christianity that you're teaching, it is not what I want my child subjected to." I left. I felt good about standing up for Don, but I felt apart from my church. I had been so active through the years and to be treated like this hurt.

I went through a period when I could not accept the fact that there was a God. Because if there was a God and a divinely ordered universe, and if homosexuality was wrong, then God didn't order the universe too well. If Rick wasn't okay, and if homosexuality wasn't okay, then there was something wrong with God for letting Rick be the way he was. Why should God put people on earth to be horribly persecuted? I felt I didn't need to look up to a God who would let that happen.

Later I directed my belligerence to church people and their narrowmindedness. Now I don't feel I have to go along with any organized religion if they're doing things I don't think are conducive to worshipping God. I can find God just sitting quietly by myself. I just can't force myself to go and sit with people who feel bad about my son.

The last time Robin was home from college, my husband Ron and I were talking about this religious thing. He was brought up Catholic, and I was not. And he feels that one of the main functions of a marriage is to bear children.

This is the second marriage for both of us. I don't know what he thinks about his sons going out and siring babies out of wedlock and living with people, and so forth. I wasn't about to get into that.

But the other night he was saying that one reason he's having trouble accepting Robin's lesbianism is because to him the purpose of a union is to procreate. And she will not be procreating. So I guess from his standpoint, with his upbringing as a Catholic, it presents more of a problem.

I'm not into Catholicism at all. And the procreation doesn't bother me one bit. I know a lot of people who are married and not having children. What's the difference if you're married and not having children, or if you're living with someone and not having children? You can hardly call them sinful.

I was watching a television show where a minister was saying that gays were an abomination. He mentioned several verses from scripture to prove it and held up a Bible. I sat there glued to my chair for awhile. That man doesn't know my son, but he used a biblical one-liner to show his hate. A chill ran down my spine as I thought about my son's being made into a "nonperson" in the name of God.

When I used to read about the Nazis in Germany who were so horrible to the Jewish people, I'd think, "Thank God we're not like that in America." But as I listened to that minister, I wasn't so sure. I thought, "What if more and more people get stirred up by people like him! Could there be a blood bath against lesbians and gays here?" For a few minutes I was filled with terror. I had to get up and vacuum the rugs to get my mind off of it.

I don't really think it could happen here—surely not. I have to think that there are enough fair-minded people in this country who would object.

RELIGIOUS THINKING IN TRANSITION

We can see from these comments that parents take it for granted that their religious leaders and associates will condemn homosexuality. But other parents have used their fears as a spur to explore the changes that are now going on. They have found more diversity than they expected.

My wife, our son and I were on a televison talk show about gay issues. A fundamentalist minister on the panel said, "According to scriptural passages, homosexuality is equivalent to murder or adultery." There was a gasp from the audience. I recall I had a flash of anger at the hurt directed at my son. When I glanced at Scott and saw that he was unmoved, even amused, my anger turned to relief and even a kind of pity for such a minister. During the audience participation period which came later, the minister won little sympathy for his cause—a claim that he had a program that could use religious conversion to change homosexuals to heterosexuals. The occasion became a powerful motivating force to become acquainted with what leaders of other religious groups were saying. Through readings I discovered that the message I heard that morning is under challenge by religious writers from many denominations. There really are winds of change at work.

In the past few years, theological thinkers have begun to review the biblical passages that condemn homosexuality as unnatural and sinful. They are realizing that the few condemnatory verses in scripture arose at a time when the authority of the father in the family and the clan was supreme and unquestioned. In those perilous Old Testament times, having children was a major priority for the survival and prosperity of the community. But knowledge of sexuality and procreation was inaccurate. It was thought that each male "seed" was a new being. They assumed that the mother only provided an incubator for the baby. Therefore, any sexual activity that "wasted the seed" was considered a threat to the tribe. Coitus interruptus, male homosexuality, or masturbation were all deemed deserving of a judgment as severe as execution.

The male heads of the families also determined the general attitudes of the clan. While they espoused heterosexuality, they were opposed to the equality of the sexes. Women were viewed as property, valued for their ability to have sons. Female children were sometimes put to death, and women had few rights. Today the majority of people in Western societies consider such beliefs as outrageous violations of human dignity.

As for homosexuality, the old patriarchs scornfully, even cruelly, rejected it, as evidenced by their practice of anal rape against enemies as a way of humiliating them. In this practice, a man was using a man as he would a woman—as an inferior to be dominated. Such practices and beliefs do not fit into our present knowledge of women or homosexual people. Neither do they fit the needs of our society.

But the old ideas die with difficulty, particularly in fundamentalist churches. However there is new hope, as theologians are now considering the scientific evidence that homosexuality is simply a natural condition for some people in all cultures. More and more of them are maintaining that the religious view of gayness should not be limited by outdated attitudes. A more generous spirit applies the universal biblical messages of loving your neighbor and being fair and nonjudgmental to all persons—gay as well as heterosexual. A better day is breaking for our gay and lesbian children as the new spirit becomes absorbed into religious life.

It is important that parents realize they no longer need to be browbeaten by the Old Testament assumptions. Many religious writers do not condemn either gay people or their parents. Parents who choose to move to full acceptance will find themselves in agreement with the enlightened ideas of many respected religious thinkers.

The issues about religion and homosexuality are complex and emotionally charged. Since many parents have experienced agony about this topic, we feel obligated to face it.

Parents who are not concerned about religious questions may wish to skip the next section. We know, however, that parents will hear about the scriptural passages condemning homosexuality. To ignore these because they are disturbing can leave parents with hurtful, unfinished emotional business. We think it is better to look the religious issue squarely in the eye.

THE FOUR PREVAILING RELIGIOUS ATTITUDES

We want to illustrate what is going on in religious thought by giving examples of actual arguments now underway.

One of the studies we found most useful was James B. Nelson's *Embodiment: An Approach to Sexuality and Christian Theology.* Nelson, a professor of Christian Ethics at the United Theological Seminary of the Twin Cities, identifies what he calls four theological positions toward homosexuality in the contemporary religious scene: (1) a rejecting-punitive attitude (homosexuality should not be accepted and should be punished), (2) a rejecting-nonpunitive attitude (homosexuality is seen as forbidden by scriptures, but homosexual persons should be treated with forgiving grace), (3) a qualified acceptance position (homosexuality is tolerable if it is deemed irreversible and if the relationship is monogamous), and (4) full acceptance (homosexuality should be placed on a par with heterosexuality and the same ethical principles should be applied to both).[2]

The Rejecting-Punitive Attitude

So God created man in His own image; in the image of God He created him; male and female created He them.... and God said unto them "Be fruitful and multiply." (Genesis 1:27, 28)

To many readers of the Bible this passage offers scriptural proof that God's natural design for humans is heterosexual union. For them this proves that any sexual expression other than heterosexuality is unnatural and sinful.

Isolated passages from the Bible are quoted by biblical literalists to establish this position. Two passages from Leviticus are direct and to the point:

> You shall not lie with a male as with a woman, it is an abomination. (Leviticus 18:22)

> If a man lie with a male as with a woman, both of them have committed an abomination; they shall be put to death, their blood is upon them. (Leviticus 21:13)

We might add in passing that Leviticus also says:

> If a man commits adultery with the wife of his neighbor, both the adulterer and adulteress shall be put to death. (Leviticus 20:10)

While it is clear that passages such as these are important to those who adopt a rejecting-punitive attitude, it is strange how they pull back from the literal punishment prescribed.

We note, too, how scriptural passages are unfairly selected to bring homosexuality under attack. Parents are often shown the passages about gays being sent to hell. Rarely are they told that the same fate awaits those who are greedy for money, who are heavy drinkers, or who have sex outside of marriage. Nor do they mention passages from Leviticus which prohibit the eating of rabbit, oysters, clams, shrimp, or pork.

It is worth noting James Nelson's comment on the selective wrath the fundamentalists reserve for homosexuality:

> Today no major contemporary theologian holds the rejecting-punitive position, and most church bodies in their formal statements have moved away from it. Yet in practice, it may still be by far the most common orientation throughout the length and breadth of the church in our society. Its theology rests on a selective Biblical literalism— selective because other moral issues are not treated with the same kind of moralism at all.[3]

Nelson himself offers some interesting speculations about this selective fixation on homosexuality and the highly charged anxiety and rage that lie behind it. For example, from a Freudian perspective, he points out that even for people whose sex life has been exclusively heterosexual, there may be homosexual feelings present even if relegated to an unconscious level. Freud's idea of reaction formation showed that one way we cope with our own unwanted impulses is by attacking them in others.[4]

Furthermore, the male-dominated tradition contains exaggerated images of masculinity that trigger strong anxiety about homosexuality among men. Homosexuality is viewed as unmanly. It threatens clear masculine gender identity, and the ground rules that establish what safe and normal male feelings are supposed to be. Any crossing of the forbidden line unleashes feelings of high danger. As Nelson puts it, the gay male seems a threat to the importance of super-masculinity, "and his very presence seems to call into question so much that many heterosexual men have sacrificed to be 'manly'."[5] In other words, many gay men refuse to give up the softer, more gentle "feminine" qualities which macho traditions have taught are "only for women." Thus anthropologists have noted the strong tendency of patriarchal cultures to define homosexuality as "the unspeakable sin" while matriarchal cultures have been very different. In the Old Testament, there is severe condemnation of male homosexuality while lesbianism is not even mentioned. It is only gay men who suffer the condemnation of the Old Testament. Yet the rejecting-punitive part of the tradition is still heard from many pulpits today.

The Rejecting-Nonpunitive Attitude

While homosexuality still provokes high levels of anger and anxiety, it is equally true that the Old Testament attitudes are being brought under question.

A first step is the emergence of a rejecting, nonpunitive position. Nelson says this is found among theologians who reject the harshness of the fundamentalists. They still operate from the assumption that homosexual relations are unnatural in that they violate the commands of the Creator. Karl Barth, a major Protestant theologian, is one who holds this view. But Barth hastens to add that the central theme of the Christian gospel is God's overwhelming grace; therefore, the homosexual person must not be condemned even though homosexuality itself must be. To the theologian, this may be seen as a generous statement. But those of us who feel that our children's homosexuality was not a choice, view this position as placing an unjustified sense of guilt and unworthiness on our sons and daughters.

The official Catholic teaching is rejecting but non-punitive, that is, "homosexual orientation (sexual attraction toward a person of the same sex) is held to be morally neutral (not sinful), but homosexual actions are objectively sinful."[6] This prescribes for homosexuals the same conditions of celibacy demanded of those who take vows for the holy orders. From our perspective, this expectation for ordinary lay people seems unrealistically severe.

The Qualified Acceptance Attitude

We can observe cautious moves toward qualified acceptance by certain Catholic thinkers. On the one hand, they feel the pull to stay within official teaching; on the other hand, they are influenced by the studies which show that homosexuality is simply a natural condition for a certain percentage of the population.

There was, for example, *The Declaration on Sexual Ethics* by the Sacred Congregation for the Doctrine of the Faith (1975). The authors distinguished between homosexuals, who are such because of "some kind of innate instinct or a pathological constitution judged to be incurable," and those homosexuals whose tendencies come from "false education, bad example, bad habits, etc." But the declaration backs away from concluding that homosexual activity is natural. Homosexual acts are held to lack a "biological creative potential" and, therefore, are "intrinsically disordered."[7]

At the same time, a number of reputable Catholic moralists are moving closer to qualified acceptance, although heterosexuality is still held to be the norm for human sexuality. They continue to refer to homosexuality as "essentially incomplete," "not normative," "not an ideal." Their argument for qualified acceptance runs like this:

> Because a homosexual orientation, for which an individual is in no way responsible, precludes heterosexual fulfillment, homosexual behavior in certain contexts is not subjectively (and perhaps even objectively) wrong for a person who is a true, constitutional, irreversible homosexual.[8]

On the basis of this new acknowledgment of the homosexual condition as irreversible, these moralists condone as an alternative to homosexual promiscuity, a "stable, faithful, loving homosexual relationship." A relationship with such qualities is accepted as "the lesser of two evils."

The Full Acceptance Attitude

Beyond qualified acceptance, there are serious moralist writers among both Catholics and Protestants who embrace full acceptance. For example, there is the statement by the English Society of Friends in its widely read *Towards A Quaker View of Sex* (1963): "One should no more deplore homosexuality than left-handedness. ... Homosexual affection can be as selfless as heterosexual affection, and, therefore, we cannot see that it is in some way morally worse."[9]

Norman Pittenger, a noted Anglican theologian, in *Time for Consent: A Christian's Approach to Homosexuality* further spells out this point of view.[10] He says that at base our sexuality means the possibility of expressing and sharing a total personal relationship in love. Gay persons need deep and lasting relationships just as do heterosexuals. Appropriate genital expression should not be denied to either. Pittenger argues that a Christian position should be developed in terms of a central ethical question: "What sexual behavior will serve to enhance, rather than inhibit and damage, the full realization of our divinely intended humanity?" The answer is sexual behavior consistent with an ethic of love—a responsible, ongoing communion with another human that involves commitment, trust, tenderness, and respect. A Christian ethic of love rules out selfish exploitation, cruelty, impersonal sex, obsession with sex, and actions done without mutual willingness. Such an ethic is equally appropriate for heterosexuals and homosexuals; therefore, there should be no double standard.

In *Homosexual Catholics: A Primer for Discussion* there is an extension of the case for full acceptance. According to this position, the norm or ideal in any relationship, regardless of gender, is justice and love. The quality of the relationship, therefore, rather than sex per se determines morality. As the authors of *Homosexual Catholics* puts it,

> Since homosexuality has been evidenced at all times and places in human history and in all known cultures to some degree, it could be interpreted as part of the divine plan. While scripture condemns homosexual activity related to lust, idol worship, rape, inhospitality, it cannot be said to condemn loving homosexual relationships between true homosexual persons. The Genesis account must be seen in light of patriarchal culture, male domination, and propagation of the Jewish race.[11]

We hasten to add that these views have not received the approval of Catholic authorities. Some authors of such views have, indeed, been silenced. The truth is, however, that ideas like these are now in the public arena competing for attention. They won't go away.

Homosexuality is not the only interpersonal issue that has been seriously rethought in recent times. New Testament attitudes towards slavery and women are cases in point. How many people, for example, find their religious leaders urging them to observe literally the following passages:

> Let all who are under the yoke of slavery regard their masters as worthy of all honor. (I Timothy 6:1)

> ... the women should keep silence in the churches. If there is anything they desire to know, let them ask their husbands at home. For it is shameful for a woman to speak in church. (I Corinthians 14:34-35)

We end this account of the full acceptance line of thought among American religious thinkers with a statement by Bishop Melvin Wheatley of the United Methodist Church:

I am an enthusiastically heterosexual male. Is my heterosexuality a virtue? A sign of righteousness? Either an accomplishment or a victory of some kind on my part? Of course not. I had nothing whatsoever to do with my being heterosexual. It is a mysterious gift of God's grace communicated through an exceedingly complex set of chemical, biological, chromosomal, hormonal, environmental, developmental factors—totally outside of my control. My heterosexuality is a gift—neither a virtue nor a sin.

What I do with my heterosexuality, however, is my personal, moral, and spiritual responsibility. My behavior as a heterosexual may, therefore, be very sinful—brutal, exploitative, selfish, promiscuous, superficial. My behavior as a heterosexual, on the other hand, may be beautiful—tender, considerate, loyal, other-centered, profound.

Precisely this same distinction between being a heterosexual and behaving as a heterosexual applies to homosexual persons, unless you and I are to be guilty of that lowest blow of all, and that is to work by double standards.

Homosexuality, quite like heterosexuality, is neither a virtue nor an accomplishment. It is a mysterious gift of God's grace communicated through an exceedingly complex set of chemical, biological, chromosomal, hormonal, environmental, developmental factors—totally outside of my homosexual friend's control. His or her homosexuality is a gift—neither a sin nor a virtue. What one does with one's homosexuality, however, is one's personal, moral, and spiritual responsibility.

Behavior as a homosexual may, therefore, be very sinful—brutal, exploitative, selfish, promiscuous, superficial. Behavior as a homosexual, on the other hand, may be beautiful—tender, considerate, loyal, other-centered, profound.

With this interpretation of the mystery that must be attributed to sexual orientation, both heterosexual and homosexual, I clearly do not believe that homosexuality is a sin.[12]

In presenting these samples of the range of religious attitudes, we realize that we have said nothing about the views of the Jewish community. We have inquired into this area enough only to say that the views among Orthodox, Conservative, and Reform Jews seem to roughly parallel the four orientations found among Christians.

PARENTS TAKING A STAND

Ultimately, parents have to work out their personal resolutions. It can be confusing to know what to do in a time of such great cultural change. Eventually, a stand must be taken. We have sympathetic appreciation for parents who struggle towards full and loving acceptance. We believe the following quotations illustrate that parents who move towards acceptance are furthering their own peace of mind and deep personal growth.

My son, Chuck, had given serious thought to becoming a minister. I was an officer in the church and was pledged to uphold the laws and regulations of the church. But when Chuck's situation came into my awareness, things began to seem very hypocritical to me. I felt a lot of resentment towards the church, realizing that he could never be ordained as a minister in that denomination.

About that time I became interested in another denomination which had a different and more generous outlook. As I thought more about it, I decided that I really didn't want to be part of an organization that made such distinctions. So I left the church, which was rather traumatic. Everybody in my family, including myself, had been very active in our old church, so to pull out, you know, did cause a few ripples. But I don't regret it at all. I'm very happy in my present situation.

This friend could tell me where anything was in the Bible that I wanted to know. I asked her where did the Bible talk about homosex-

uality. She told me, and I showed it to Robin. "You know," I said, "the Bible says it is wrong." At least I interpreted it to mean that homosexuality is wrong. There was no question in my mind. It bothered me a lot.

But Robin said, "There are so many things in the Bible that are totally obsolete and no longer apply today—like the attitude towards women. Those things are the outdated remnants of an ancient society. The fundamentalists and the moral majority don't abide by those things either. They shrug them off and just say 'Oh well, those don't count.' Another thing the Bible absolutely forbids is masturbation. Now the sex experts tell us that ninety-nine percent of males and a very high percentage of females have masturbated. It's no big deal: it's normal and healthy. So again, the Bible's rules are shrugged off as obsolete, due to better, more realistic information."

You might say that if God accepts people as they are, then we need to accept people as they are. If we condemn people, in the name of religion, then we're assuming God's responsibilities. If God is the judge, then let God do the judging.

So I think that the worst thing we can do is to be narrow-mindedly judgmental. Being judgmental about people and their sexual behavior is not a very religious thing to do. I think most of us have all we can do to manage our own lives, let alone make decisions about how other people ought to manage theirs.

Judging people and feeling superior may be more sinful than anyone's so-called sexual misbehavior. How do we know what's in other people's minds and hearts when it comes to sexual practices that are between consenting and loving adults?

I know that, because of their religious orientation, many parents feel strongly that gayness is wrong. What can they do?

For one thing, they should do some reading other than materials from their own denomination. Read other religious philosophers who really bring together the teachings of the great religious masters of all times. For example, think of the teachings of Jesus Himself. Over and over again He preached that the Kingdom of God is within. I see this as meaning that we have an inner teacher. The inner teacher is always saying "Go into the secret place" which means the inner place where

God is within us. We can reach that inner teacher through meditation and prayer, quiet and peace.

I really believe we can get answers from within ourselves, because this inner teacher is our own best self and our own true center.

LEARNING FROM OUR RELIGIOUS DIFFERENCES

In the parents' group we had to confront the diverse religious backgrounds of our members. Among our members there were Roman Catholics, Jews, people from various Protestant denominations, Unitarians, Ethical Culturists, and freethinkers. Our ability to handle this religious diversity was a fundamental challenge and test of our own basic values.

We worked together to find ways that honored the right of each person to hold the religious convictions that fit his or her needs. Some of our most productive activities came from communication with gay support groups in denominations that are beginning to serve their lesbian and gay members. We opened ourselves to learning by handling our religious diversity constructively.

There seems to be a connection between acceptance of sexual diversity and acceptance of religious diversity. As parents of gay people, we are suggesting that Americans can accept diverse forms of sexual expression (always following the principle that freedom of choice bars any form of harm to others) just as Americans permit freedom of religious choice. By asking the American people to accept the hitherto rejected gay segment of society, we are simply asking that one of the hallowed American traditions be extended to gay people: the tradition of *e pluribus unum* (out of many, one).

Americans developed that principle to make it possible for the diverse groups who came here in search of freedom of conscience to live together peacefully. The underlying social gamble was that tolerance and acceptance could lead to mutual enrichment. It is a principle that has always required stern discipline, embracing, as it does, the right to differ tempered by a willingness to give a respectful hearing to dissenting opinions and ways of living.

We think that respect for the American principle of pluralism should be extended to the diverse sexual orientations that are a part of American reality, and that are a part of human reality. As folk singer Holly Near put it, "...once felt, if only for a moment, we know the taste of what could be—people sharing a world enriched by their differences, and no one being asked to give up the best of who they are."[13]

If we risk listening carefully to those who seek to combine their gay nature with their deep religious convictions, we might find it a fresh source of spiritual growth. We end with a statement by a young gay man from Dignity, an organization of Catholic gay people with whom we cooperate. He shares the anguish of a personal question: How, in the name of religion, can he be asked to deny one of the deepest truths of his nature—his homosexuality?

He works towards a resolution by contemplating a statement from Mahatma Gandhi: "Inside each of us God has written His clearest messages."

Gandhi was one of those remarkable people appearing from time to time on our planet, whose teachings and lives have a profound impact. Gandhi said, "There is no other God than truth. I worship God as truth only." And "To me, in its largest sense, religion means self-realization or knowledge of self."

Those of us who are gay should be able to appreciate what Gandhi was saying. Despite the conviction of many religious leaders that they know the truth about homosexuality, we who are gay know that their easy answers just do not make sense to our reality.

How many of these religious leaders with the "answers" know even the most fundamental facts about homosexuality? How many of them have really listened to our stories?

The particular interpretation these people give to certain Bible passages conflicts with the nature God has given us. It is the God of the Bible who has created us with the gift of loving others of the same gender in an emotional, spiritual, and sexual way. Many of us, in order to survive as sane humans, have had to ultimately reject the condemnatory statements of leaders who act as though they are wiser than Gandhi, Jesus, or the Buddha.

To find answers, to come close to the truth, we have to practice the kind of religion Gandhi practices. We have to look into ourselves, into our nature. It is inside each of us that God has written the clearest messages.

If we are seeking the truth, we also know that it is not easy seeing beyond the homophobia inside us. We have to seek, to look within, if we want to follow the path of Jesus, the Buddha, and Gandhi. They were not wedded to doctrines and dogmas, but to the pursuit of truth.[14]

NOTES FOR CHAPTER 4

[1]Letha Dawson Scanzoni, "Putting a Face on Homosexuality," *The Other Side,* Issue 149 (February 1984) pp. 9-10. Reprinted with permission from *The Other Side* magazine, 300 W. Apsley Street, Philadelphia, PA 19144.

[2]James B. Nelson, *Embodiment: An Approach to Sexuality and Christian Theology* (New York: Pilgrim Press, 1978).

[3]Ibid. p. 189.

[4]Ibid. p. 202.

[5]Ibid. p. 204.

[6]Robert Nugent, Jeannine Gramick and Thomas Oddo, *Homosexual Catholics: A New Primer for Discussion* (Washington, DC: Dignity, Inc., 1980) p. 3.

[7]Ibid.

[8]Ibid. pp. 5-6.

[9]*Towards a Quaker View of Sex: An Essay by a Group of Friends* (London: Friends House, 1963) pp. 26, 41.

[10]Norman Pittenger, *Time for Consent: A Christian's Approach to Homosexuality* (London: SCM Press, Ltd., 1976). See especially Chapter 3, "What Is Man?"; Chapter 11, "An Ethics for Homosexuals," and Chapter 12, "A Religious Epilogue."

[11]Nugent, op. cit. p. 6.

[12]From an address by Bishop Melvin Wheatley (ret.) with his permission.

[13]Quote by Holly Near, written for the song "Unity" on *Journeys* (RR405). Redwood Records. Used with permission.

[14]Kevin O'Shea, *Dignity Newsletter,* 3, no. 3 (April 1, 1983).

chapter 5

Changing
Inner Perceptions

I would like to get to the point where I can feel that her homosexuality is as natural for her as heterosexuality is for me. I'd like to get to the point where homosexuality isn't all that important in our life with Mary. It won't be easy to do, and I don't know if it'll come to that. But I hope so.

People ask me, "Does it bother you that your son has chosen that kind of life?" He's no masochist. He'd never "choose" it. It's a hard world out there. It's hard for everyone, and it's extremely hard for gays and lesbians. The gay life style involves a lot more responsibility and hazards than the heterosexual life style. Don did not choose to be gay, but he did choose to live as a gay man with pride.

Pat never really blossomed until after she came out about her homosexuality. Her total personality wasn't evident until she knew we had accepted her for what she was. After that she could relax and be herself around us. That was a joy for us to receive.

It's sad for me to see the pain, the unhappiness, the degradation, the shunning that our gay children have to go through just because they have a different life style. I believe—I know—that some day our kids can live in a happier world where they will be judged for their deeds and not their sexual orientation.

When we first came face-to-face with our children's gayness, our antiquated value system generated a distressing conflict. Our inner voices told us that being gay or lesbian was unmentionable, scary, sinful, and sick. These beliefs were as deeply entrenched in us as the automatic way we washed dishes or drove a car.

Up until the moment we found out, we had seen our children as healthy, bright, normal, not in any way like our ideas about gay people. Which outlook was correct? We thought we couldn't give up either perception. But we certainly couldn't reconcile them either. To try to get out of this conflict we could have turned our backs on the homosexuality of our children. But we would still have remained in irreconcilable conflict. Or we could rethink and change our inner perceptions.

The parents interviewed chose to go through a 180-degree change in their perception of their children's sexual nature. Their inward journey was sometimes discouragingly slow; for most it required enormous effort, and for all it took courage. They started out seeing society as being okay and their child as flawed. They ended up seeing their child as okay, but society as flawed.

Some parents experienced the whole range of negative reactions that we will report on in this chapter. Others traveled through only a few. Each had a different time schedule. The personality, personal experiences, and background of each person created a unique reaction within the growing process. No parent traveled through easily. There were many setbacks for each parent as the new learning process gradually became more and more of a comfortable response.

Feelings were the key to opening up the inner world. It was important for parents to acknowledge the depth of whatever negative feelings they had. When these were faced and gradually dropped, they made room for new perceptions that fit their children.

While honesty of feelings is important for adjustment, parents should avoid venting unrestrained frustrations on their gay children. A good friend serves this purpose far better.

Parents who tried to change without going through the work of facing all their negative feelings were disappointed. Such feelings cannot be willed away by good intentions. A few people, very shocked at negative feelings towards their own children, sugarcoated them. When we heard parents say they had no problems with their children's gayness, we wondered if they might be denying very real problems. Such denial could lead to a stagnation of grief.

We are sure that gay and lesbian children are often disappointed with the negative reaction that their parents first show. But early reactions are not a reliable indication of whether parents will move towards and beyond acceptance. A much better indicator is a willingness to open themselves to new information and to maintain contact with their child.

OPENING UP TO FEELINGS

In recalling their early feelings and experiences, many of the parents we interviewed told us that for days and sometimes weeks after learning of their child's gayness, they were consumed with the news. Homosexuality filled the mind and was the thought for the day. For most there was a sense of tragedy, of loss, and for a time, an all-consuming pain. The very foundation on which their daily lives was built felt shaky and insecure.

After reading the letter that Mary wrote telling us she was gay, I couldn't think of anything else. I went about my daily work, but the thought of Mary's being gay was never out of my mind for an instant. I had difficulty sleeping at night, and the very second that I would wake, the thought would be with me. Over and over I kept thinking, "What are we going to do?"

The word homosexual seemed planted across my forehead for days after Matt told us he was gay. It was the first thing I thought about in the morning and the last thing I thought about at night. I even dreamed about it.

Grief

These early feelings and actions were usually a part of an encompassing grief. Many parents were surprised at the intensity and length of time it took to grieve. One mother compared her grief to that of parents whose child has died. Isolation and a lack of help magnified their sense of desolation.

I was devastated. I can't even describe my feelings. I was just so numb for awhile.

Sometimes I even thought it would have been easier if my daughter were dead. I didn't think this very long or very often, but it does show how upset I was.

One of the most painful parts was facing the issue of a perfect family. It was very important to my self-esteem that I see myself as a VERY GOOD MOTHER with capital letters. And VERY GOOD MOTHERS raise perfect children. For awhile a gay son was far from being my idea of a perfect child.

I thought, "I'll never have grandchildren from James. James will never bring home a lovely girl and say, 'Well, this is the one, Mom.'
There was a certain amount of grief for awhile—grief that my dreams were shattered. I didn't have them written down, but they were there, somewhere in the back of my mind, and they had been killed.

Anger

Anger was not uncommon for parents. It struck in various ways. Sometimes it was directed at the child. Many times the son's or daughter's lover got the brunt of it. At times anger was veiled, but often it was direct, and parents said and did things they later regretted. This early anger masked their frustration, fear, and hurt. It signaled to parents that they had a lot of work to do. They sensed that something was drastically amiss, but at this level they often did not understand exactly what that was.

I was filled with both anger at being told and gratitude that she had not told us earlier. Then I would get angry that she hadn't trusted us enough to tell us. My thinking and feelings made no sense at all.

I didn't stop to think of her pain. I thought of myself more than I did of Sarah. It was all too new for me. We were getting ready for the wedding of our son, Joe, at the time that Sarah chose to let us know she was gay. I thought she used poor timing, and I was angry at her for that. I wondered why she picked that particular time to tell us, and I thought it was terribly unkind of her.

We had some pretty harsh words over the phone several times. I think Sarah expected too much too soon. One statement Sarah made was, "I want you to be as happy for Sheryl and me as you are for Joe finding someone to love." Mark and I almost simultaneously blurted out, "How can we be happy about that? Find a man to love. Then we'll be happy." That was a very cruel thing. I can't speak for my husband, but I was trying to hurt her as she had hurt me. It's nothing to be proud of, a revelation like that, but it's the truth. After that there was no communication for some time.

My son had a friend who told him how his parents reacted when they found out they had a gay son. That boy's mother said to him, "You got that at school. I didn't bring you up to be that way. You just leave that right where you got it." She said it over and over to him.

And his father would say, "God made Adam and Eve. He didn't make Adam and Steve."

After all this time I still hate John's first lover with a passion. I could still punch him if I had the chance. It wasn't his fault, but I hated that S.O.B.

Sadness

For awhile most parents were sad and depressed. Tears were frequent. For some, day-to-day activities became difficult to perform.

I just went to pieces—inside, not outside—because Tom still didn't know. I thought, "I can't go to work." Then I'd think, "I have to go to work. The bills are going to accumulate whether Jerry's gay or not. The world is going to go on too."

Mark and I did not know how to handle it. We didn't know where we were going to go with it. We didn't know how to act. I was hurt and confused. I wondered what I had done to deserve this.

It's been six months now, and I still find myself crying. At first I cried all the time. I'd be at work and all at once I'd tear up. I wondered if I would ever get over that sad feeling.

It hurt so bad there were times when I was sorry I had to wake up and face the day. I often wished I could die.

I have periods when I accept this very nicely. Other times I sink into depression. Then I find I just have to get away from thinking about Marilyn's being gay. I don't want to think or talk about it. But sometimes I feel I just have to talk. Right now, for instance, I'm finding that talking is good.

Loneliness

At first most parents thought their families were the only ones who had a gay child. Some felt lonely and had trouble relating to old friends. Even the most common social interactions became uncomfortable.

I felt so alone. I cried, and I didn't know why. I thought, "How am I going to live through this?" I'm a single parent and didn't know where to turn.

It was really hard for us to enjoy any kind of social contact with people for awhile. We got so tired of hearing people ask if Tony had a steady girl friend. Those kinds of questions were hard. So we withdrew inside ourselves.

Guilt

Guilt implies that something is wrong, and that someone must be made to take the blame. Parents of lesbians or gays in our society are often made to feel like criminals, and frequently they are all too willing to assume a criminal status. Many parents interviewed also felt guilty and searched for a culprit to share their presumed failing. They blamed their child, the child's lover, someone in the child's past, or the other parent. Guilt and blame are a natural part of any loss. But such reactions, if continued too long, can trap parents in a self-destructive pattern.

It just stands to reason that mothers are usually closer to their sons in the early years than fathers are. Now they have found out that gay men have no more problems because of this than nongay ones. That whole idea was wrong. But I suffered a lot of guilt. I thought that the family was the cause of homosexuality and that the mother was a big part of that cause. I was quick to condemn myself. You know, everyone has an opinion about homosexuality, but nobody really knows. There are a lot of hurtful ideas going around.

Now I don't see our family as different from other families. The troubles that we had, even though they were painful, were the usual troubles that many families have.

Even now when I think of how Greg was when he was a little boy, I feel guilty. I wish I could have helped him more. I wish I could have been more accepting.

I was plagued with feelings of guilt like, "Were we a bad family? Were we bad parents? Was I a bad mother?"

Failure

For many, producing children who did not fit easily into society also produced a loss of their feelings of competence as men and women. For awhile some parents were left with a feeling of failure that was intense.

When I was younger I felt okay about myself. But after Roy told us he was gay, for a while I thought I was a failure as a man.

My mother was a drug addict and she abused me. But I thought she was a better mother than I was because she didn't raise a gay child.

Shame

Feelings of shame engulfed many of the interviewed parents as they began to deal with the taboo that accompanies homosexuality in this society. They were often unaware of how strong this taboo was until they were faced with it in their own family.

There was an added problem. Parents were usually in their forties and fifties before being confronted with society's prejudice against their children. Settled into a way of life, they were confident that they knew how to act in this complicated world. Suddenly they felt they were members of a minority group being openly attacked, and they had not developed the defenses to cope with this onslaught.

I worried about what people would say. Would they laugh? Would they look down on us? We didn't tell anybody for quite a while.

It sounds ridiculous to be so concerned about what people think. Why should that worry anybody that much? But it does. It seems to intimidate a lot of parents, and it certainly intimidated me. I thought, "What if people gasped! What if they whispered behind my back! What if! What if! What if!"

There weren't many books in the library about homosexuality, and I couldn't even go get them if they were there. I wondered how I could check out such books without looking like I had a gay son.

For the first time in my life I was ashamed of one of my children. I had always thought my kids were better than other kids that I knew. My feeling of superiority quickly vanished.

Fears of Catastrophe

Sometimes parents were filled with overwhelming and frightening thoughts. They imagined catastrophic happenings or pictured their children as being abnormal.

There is an in-law in the family who is so far to the right that he is entirely capable of going to the bar association and reporting her. Her career could be ruined.

I knew she was going to be a schoolteacher. I also knew what people think about a homosexual teaching school. I knew what society thinks about gays, period. I thought, "She's going to have a miserable life."

For awhile I even thought of my son as a pervert.

Questions About Own Sexuality

The homophobia that most parents started out with often caused them to doubt their own heterosexuality, the quality of their role modeling, and/or the quality of their genes. Often there was a fear of having "opposite-gender" traits. They examined their behavior in detail and worried that anything other than total societal conformity might have contributed to their child's being gay. Some even wondered if they themselves were somehow latent homosexuals.

Most parents have picked up mixed messages about what constitutes an ideal parent. We have been caught in a bind by the changing standards for parenting. Since no parent perfectly fulfills the ideals that our society imposes, parents of gays have an almost built-in case for feeling unsure about the example they have set.

Almost any caring mother, single or married, may ask, "Was I too strong? Was I being seductive when I was cuddling my son? Was I castrating when I gave him advice or asked him to help me with the dishes? Did the decisions I had to make somehow make men appear weak?"

A father might ask, "Does enjoying the company of other males make me partially gay? Am I too domestic because I like to cook? Should I have insisted that my daughter wear dresses more often? Was I wrong to let my son drop out of Boy Scouts? Should I have been a 'tough guy' like John Wayne who rarely showed his feelings? If I had been home more would my child be gay?"

While this was a difficult revelation for them to make, some parents were willing to discuss the doubts that crossed their minds about their own sexual orientation.

I think we all feel love toward members of our own sex, especially if they have any trouble. I often want to hold my friends when they're in sorrow. To love another woman is very natural to me, but to love her sexually is not my norm.

I think anybody who finds out there is someone gay in the family is going to stop and think, "If the situation had been right would I have been that way?" I started examining my sexual feelings towards other women and realized I'd never looked at any woman and had sexual thoughts. So I didn't see how I could possibly be gay. Jerry knew he was gay when he was in high school; but when I was that age I wasn't looking at girls. I was looking at boys. These are the kinds of thoughts that probably go through everybody's mind.

When you are faced with the homosexuality of your child, you're faced with something you don't quite understand. I wondered if I could be homosexual too. I have examined and questioned myself on it. Finally I decided that people are really socially conditioned from the time they are little to be heterosexual. But some people just cannot be heterosexual; for them the conditioning just doesn't work.

I was a real tomboy when I was a little girl, and I guess I had more "masculine" traits than some girls. But I've never had any homosexual attraction even in my fantasies. Maybe if I were in prison and there were no other sexual outlets, I might have some sexual interest in women. I can understand in an intellectual way how a lesbian feels, but from a gut level I can't.

For awhile there I wondered if homosexuality ran in the family. I have a brother who is gay and a son who is gay. I thought, "Am I sure I'm totally straight?" It very definitely bothered me for awhile. Now I've reached the point where I see no reason to question my own sexuality. I don't think it's bad to have a gay son or brother anymore.

MOVING TOWARDS ACCEPTANCE

As parents learned to shed their guilt and become more relaxed about their parenting, they became aware of their own inner prejudices and experienced a desire to be rid of them. They realized their daughter or son felt pain too and was like them in her or his needs, wants, and desires. In a way there was a reversal of roles, as parents sought help from their children. From this, most parents developed a new understanding and pride in their child. Homosexuality was put in its proper perspective as being a natural variation of sexuality.

Commitment to Child Renewed

The common denominator among parents was a sense of permanent involvement and commitment to their child. They did not want any separation. Even in the depths of their early grief, there were strong expressions of parental concern and loyalty.

I could never turn my back on any of my children. I don't know what they would have to do for me to throw up my hands and give up on them. My love for Dan was greater than my anxiety about his homosexuality. The best way I can say it is that for me love conquered all. I knew I would stick by him no matter what.

At first I figured that we would remain close. He would still be a part of our life, but I wasn't sure if I could be a part of his. I wondered about going to visit him and if we would get to know his friends. It worried me because I didn't want to feel separate from my son in any way. Time has proved this worry to be totally wrong. Harry and I are as close to Eric as we ever were.

Accepting Reality of Child's Gayness

When parents were able to accept the reality of having a gay child, their despondency lifted noticeably. As they turned and faced the reality of their situation, they found it was not as bad as they first feared. The welfare of their child resumed its high priority on their list of concerns.

Once I accepted the fact that Dan was gay, I had a lot of fears about it. Oh, not about how I would handle it, but that he might get hurt. He might have some experience that was detrimental to him mentally or physically or in some other way. I was more worried about his well-being than I was about anything else.

We have accepted Mike's homosexuality. We gave up all those unrealistic dreams. This freed us from false hopes. Mike doesn't have to go through that constant battle between what he is and what we thought he should have been.

Once I got the obstacle of cause out of the way, I started putting the pieces together. My anger left, and our parent-child relationship became comfortable. I didn't feel disappointment that he was gay instead of straight. That he will probably never give me grandchildren doesn't bother me, because that's just the way his life is going to be.

There's a certain amount of relief on my husband's part as well as mine. I don't think his and Robin's relationship has changed much. It might be a little better because my husband is no longer wondering what could be wrong. He now knows why there was a barrier between them.

I remember that one time he said to Robin, "I'm going to take you out and buy you some feminine clothes." So they went shopping, and he spent hundreds of dollars on all these clothes for her. Most of them she has never had on her body. She went along with it just to appease him because she cares so much about him.

Even though I can't change the fact that she's a lesbian, in the back of my mind I still hope she can find some guy. But it's a relief to know about this because I used to wonder why she was not dating much, or why she hardly ever wore dresses. Now I know why things are happening, and the atmosphere is conducive to talking it over.

Confronting Inner Prejudice

Parents have to live with the fact that they rarely questioned and may have participated in prejudicial remarks. As members of this homophobic society it was not at all unusual for parents to recall laughing at gay jokes, agreeing with negative comments, and even making such comments themselves.

At the intermission of a performance of Hamlet I began talking about homosexuality, and of all things, I said to my daughter, "I find homosexuality repulsive. I can't imagine a man loving another man."

And I'm sure she must have thought, "Oh my God! How will I ever tell Mom if that's the way she feels?"

People have to learn. There was a time when I was in a skit that involved the problems of homosexuals, and we laughed because one of the fellows cut up so much. I think back to how I laughed about it. I wouldn't do that now. I wouldn't even think the skit was funny now.

I never did like to be in the presence of any homosexuals. When I was young, I avoided them. I showed my distaste. I feel a guilt about that now.

Transition: Subtle Prejudice. As the learning process continues, outward prejudice can be replaced by a subtle prejudice. This change signals that parents are moving away from their early ideas and into a more accepting attitude. In this interim period, parents often think of their child as being handicapped or less than fully normal.

Sometimes without realizing it, I compare my gay child to a child who has a handicap like blindness or deafness.

You could say if I was really accepting I wouldn't care who knew it. Since I still care about some people's knowing, I would say I am not 100 percent accepting. I still sometimes see Jean as a handicapped child. When I realize this about myself, I do feel bad. But I'm having a hard time letting go of the feeling.

Realization: Desire to Change. We found another common thread among parents who adjusted and faced their prejudice. They sensed their child could not change. They knew they were the ones who would have to change.

I don't know how much unhappiness Mary has had. I don't even know if I could bear to know. I can't shield her from the rest of the world, but I can be sure that I don't cause her any future pain.

I felt bad about my feelings. I got to thinking about it, and realized I didn't even know where my ideas came from. I decided I had to do something to wipe away what I thought about her being gay.

Action: Giving Up Guilt. After accepting the reality of gayness in the family and their own prejudice, these parents began to see how their guilt feelings were preventing them from changing themselves. They had to let that guilt move to a back burner in order to get out of the bind.

We have been brainwashed that if we have a child who is different in any way, then the parents are automatically at fault. Parents should not assume any guilt because no crime has been committed. I don't think parents are the cause. I don't see anything wrong with homosexuality anyway.

As parents we have a set of expectations for all our children. Then the children grow up, and somehow they just don't meet all those expectations. They have ideas of their own. I think parents have to come to terms with that. Some of us let go better than others.

Changing the Focus from Parent to Child

Awareness of Child's Pain. Parents have glimpses of the child's pain from the first. But until some healing occurs, they are too preoccupied to empathize deeply with their child's difficulties. As the initial grief eases, the pain their son or daughter experienced comes more and more into the foreground. Some parents have had to face the possibility that their child may have seriously considered suicide.

We know of no parents who died because of finding out they have a gay child. What we do know is that some gay people in our community have chosen to die because of a lack of support. To have a life end because that person is gay or lesbian is an abomination and an irreplaceable loss.

If I knew then what I know now, I would have raised a much healthier son. He would never have felt ashamed—or at least I would have done my utmost to keep him from feeling ashamed. I would have catered more to the things he showed interest and ability in. I would have made him feel proud of his accomplishments.

Sometimes I think about all those years when I thought she was heterosexual. It must have been hard for her.

This is something Mary has lived with since a very early age. I've heard from a friend of Mary's that she tried desperately, over a long period of time, to change. She was even engaged at one time several years ago. She told me that for awhile she figured if society couldn't accept her being gay that she would try marriage. Thank goodness she realized it wouldn't work and broke off the engagement after about six months. I think it was very wise on her part. There would have been a lot of unhappiness and probably a divorce. He is a fine young man, and Mary knew she would have caused him a good deal of pain. She cared enough for him not to hurt him.

I don't want to say I'm overjoyed that my child is gay. I don't think any of us are glad that our children will probably have a difficult time. But it's good to see that my son has found a place for himself; that he is in a world he is comfortable with and where he feels completely at ease. When he was trying to fit into the heterosexual world, he felt he wasn't making it, and was seriously depressed. I was really worried about him. I think sometimes young people commit suicide over this. They feel they have failed to meet their family's and society's standards and that the impulses they have are completely wrong. I see Chris as being satisfied now, and it's a relief for me to see him happy.

My daughter told me that when she was in high school, she was so depressed she thought of just walking slowly across a busy street so she'd be killed. This shocked me more than her telling me she was a lesbian. I was really upset about it.

In one of our talks Eric indicated that when he had worked at a music camp one summer, he had thought he'd be better off swimming out and drowning himself. Then he thought about it and decided we'd rather have him alive and homosexual than not alive. Learning about this was almost more than I could handle.

I assured him that he was right, and that whatever he was, we'd rather have him alive. Later I kept thinking about what would have happened if we had gotten a call telling us Eric had drowned. I kept telling myself that would have hurt worse, that I really hadn't experienced the worst that could happen. And, you know, that kept me going. At least I still had Eric.

Awareness of Child's Needs and Wants. Once the parents are aware of the pain their child has experienced, they are then free to understand the child's needs, desires, and wants. There is a return to the old familiar and comfortable relationship, but with an added dimension. Parents can step aside and see their son or daughter as a young adult.

In my experience with my son, I see that his biggest hurdle, emotionally, was coming out. Since doing that he seems so in control of himself. He seems in balance.

Lately I've come to the conclusion that Mary's feelings for Sheryl are as deep and sincere as mine are for Mark. I don't see how such feelings could be all that wrong. Love is love no matter which way you go.

I just want them to be happy. I think people need each other. I don't care what type of relationship it is, everyone needs someone to feel close to.

At first I thought being gay was shameful and perverted, but now I think Herb is fascinating. He's going to live a different kind of life. The life style is interesting, and some things about it are admirable. He lives a lot more in today's world than I do. I think my life would be happier if I could do that.

She's happy with her situation, and I'm satisfied with that. If I had to watch her suffer I wouldn't like that at all. Most of us really want our children to be fulfilled and happy.

Accepting the Lover and Displays of Affection

One of the last actions that parents are able to accept is overt physical affection between people of the same sex. It took a lot of peeling away of the homophobic onion skin before parents were able to approve of physical affection between their gay child and his or her lover. They spent hours on family rules concerning this issue. They had difficulty accepting such innocuous actions as hugging, patting, and kissing. Parents worried extensively about sleeping arrangements when gay couples visited.

Gay and lesbian children can help parents with this problem through a gentle educational procedure. It helps for the children to talk to the parents about the sexual nature of gays and lesbians. In many cases, just answering questions as positively as possible is enough. When parents understand the similarities between the sexual lives of gays and nongays, they are better able to accept the differences.

After parents think about and assimilate a concept about the sexuality of their children, they are ready to see open affection. All of this happens in small increments. If children expect too much too soon they will be disappointed. But most parents, whose children persistently and lovingly refuse to deny their sexual and coupling nature, lose much of their feeling of discomfort in the presence of physical affection.

I have to admit that even now when I see heterosexuals holding hands or kissing in public, I pay less attention to it than I would if they were homosexuals.

I feel uncomfortable seeing Jean kiss Cathy. I hope I'll get over this feeling. I know it's unfair, because I don't feel that way when I see straight couples doing the same thing. I try not to feel like this, but it's hard not to.

I've never seen any affection between Mary and Sheryl when they're around us. I think that would be difficult for me, the first time anyway. Perhaps after a while I'll be able to handle it better. For now I try not to think of the sexual aspect of their relationship. While it's hard for me to accept, I don't really think it's wrong on their part. I'm sure they're serious in their commitment.

Absorbing Strength from Child

Children can teach parents about gayness in many ways, not the least of which is the example they set. As the parents become the students instead of the teachers, they are comforted by the character and self-assurance of their child.

I have such admiration for Rachel's character and personality, that I knew if she felt this way, it wasn't immoral in her mind. And if it wasn't immoral in her mind, then it wasn't in my mind either.

One friend did ask me, "Don't you really wish that he was straight?" and I can very honestly say, "No. I am thrilled that I am even in the same family with this young man."

If he were in great emotional distress because of being gay, then I would certainly see that he had good counseling. But since he isn't, I feel totally at ease about the whole thing. And I feel very strongly that if he does have problems of any kind along the way, they probably won't have anything to do with his homosexuality. His sexuality is not segregated from the rest of him.

Finding Renewed Pride

As inner perception permanently changes, parents spontaneously speak of pride in their gay son or daughter. They are aware of the courage shown by all these daughters and sons who have made a place for themselves in a hostile world.

I think Gary is strong and can handle being gay pretty well. Believe it or not, I also think we gave him that. We gave him a stable home to grow up in, and there wasn't any question but that he was loved. When he came to tell us he was gay, he wasn't really worried that we would kick him out.

Don is so knowledgeable. I feel a sense of pride about what he's doing. He's working with the people in Dignity to help gays and lesbians who are Catholic. He's helping to wash away a lot of pain. It's a slow process, but at least it's starting. I think we can say there are clear skies ahead. I don't know if it will happen in our lifetime, or even in Don's lifetime. But—maybe in our grandchildren's lifetime—lesbians and gays will be accepted.

Linda has dedication, feelings, and concerns. She fulfills her responsibility, always has. She feels a closeness to the family and corresponds with us. She sends birthday cards, and she telephones, and that sort of thing. She is negotiation chairman for her union and is doing a good job. She has been quoted in the paper. She doesn't jump into things with the brashness of youth, but rather she studies things through very carefully. I am most proud of her.

I am proud of how Greg has handled himself. He chose a healthy way to enter the homosexual world. He has selected partners who are supportive. He demands that he be accepted for what he is. He refuses to hide.

Learning to Laugh

Humor is a great healer for parents who are working through their homophobic perceptions. Laughing about a situation causes our catastrophic thoughts to assume less importance and to loosen their hold on us.

Parents are often able to see the ridiculous part of some of their early ideas. One group of parents had a good laugh when they found the only thing they had in common was that they all drove Volkswagens. In the middle of a particularly trying conversation, one of the fathers said, "Sometimes we sound just like a soap opera."

Letting Go

As parents continued their work, they let go of a lot of the old dreams and ideas. They lost that vague sense of being responsible for all their son's or daughter's problems and changes, and chose not to assume guilt. This stage was a good time, a hopeful time, a time of growth for both parent and child.

Before I knew he was gay, he was keeping his distance from me and the rest of the family. But since we've known, everything has been running smoothly. I don't know how his life will evolve, or where he will ultimately choose to live. But I don't think that, because of us, he will choose to live far away.

We let each of our children go their own way. We never tried to hold them back. We did the best we could up to a point, and then our lives were ours and their lives were theirs. All of us have hopes for our children, but you can carry that only so far; then they have to go their own way.

I think there are disturbed elements in every human being. In every family there are disturbed elements and in every marriage there are disturbed elements. Ours had some of those too.

At first I felt guilty about not being the perfect parent. But I was doing the best I could, and our son has turned out to be a wonderful person. He's a child I'm proud of. He's contributing to the world. He's helping people who are suffering, and he's hurting nobody. His life style is one I think people could learn from, including myself. I feel that his sexual orientation isn't all that much of a disappointment anymore, if it's a disappointment at all.

Getting There: Placing Homosexuality in the Proper Perspective

The hard work has paid off when parents have no questions about what the real problem regarding homosexuality is. They know it is society's pervasive and unreasonable fear about gayness that causes the damage. They long for society to change and some of them will move towards becoming a force in helping that change take place.

I see her life style as perfectly okay. I still think it's inconvenient in our society. It's unfair that our society penalizes gays and their families. But that surely isn't Kate's fault. I want society to change, not Kate, and I'm working to do just that.

You don't have to have a gay child to have problems with your children. There are many things that you go through with them that are traumatic. Having a gay child is just one of the things. I think that outlook has helped me accept Rachel. I try to look at our family—and the things we've been through—as a whole, and I realize that this is just one more of the many things that can happen when you have children.

TAKING THE STEP BEYOND

After examining and reaffirming the relationship with their son or daughter, many parents became realistically aware of what their child would have to face. They began to see their child as part of a larger group that is unfairly treated. Each felt that just as his or her own child deserved civil rights, understanding and love, so did all gays and lesbians. As their own child deserved to be judged on merit and individual effort, so did all gay persons. Parents realized that gays and lesbians are like themselves with the only difference being in sexual orientation. Many parents committed themselves to the work of eliminating homophobia wherever they found it.

Widening the Focus

With their developing empathy for the feeling of being in a minority position, parents experienced and understood the deep need of lesbians and gays to live with pride. A major connection had been made. No longer could parents view gayness as a life style that was "out there." Instead, it would now be a part of their day-to-day existence.

It dawned on me that Karen had gone through a period of thinking that we'd be better off without her. I began to feel something for those young people whose folks kick them out and won't accept them. I felt anger at the parents, and I felt so much sorrow for the children. You hear these suicide statistics and think, "What kind of parent could do that to a child knowing that it might cause the child to commit suicide?"

Sally chose to go with her nature and not fight it. Otherwise, I think she would have continued to be miserable and depressed indefinitely. Why should gay or lesbian people be miserable because they have been told to deny something that doesn't hurt anybody? Many of them have told me that being gay was their nature, and they either go with it or be unhappy. I think it is immoral not to go with your natural sexual tendencies as long as you're responsible.

I had an experience that helped me understand the pain of being a member of an "undesirable" minority—it helped me understand what gays go through.

I went to a New Year's Day open house with my son shortly after he had come out to us. Everyone there was gay except Lois and me. I was the only heterosexual male.

For some reason, the gay men were suspicious of me and wouldn't talk to me. There was this invisible barrier between us. They couldn't seem to cross it, and I didn't know how to. It was an eerie feeling. Maybe I unconsciously contributed to the barrier.

It was an enlightening situation. I saw things from the viewpoint of being a minority. It opened my eyes to a lot of things—not just about gay people, but about the feelings of any minority. I got a terrific insight that day.

The statistics say that one in ten persons is gay—perhaps even more. As a high school teacher, I know that in every class I have, there is someone who is gay. One of the saddest things is that no one can help them.

I am also aware of the ridicule that young people, who are not sure of their sexual identity, go through. One of the favorite things my high school students do is to accuse one another of being gay. It's just a constant thing. Faggot is the big name they call each other when they're in junior high. There's a lot of that in high school too. I am sensitive to how that makes young people feel when they are in the midst of learning about themselves. It has to be difficult.

Recognizing That Society's View Is the Real Problem

While parents were in the process of shedding their misinformation, there was a gradual unfolding of how unfair this society's view on homosexuality is. After a time they knew without question what the real problem was and is. It is not with homosexuality per se; it is with what happens to gays and lesbians in our society.

How I wish people could realize that just because a person's life style is different, it is not necessarily wrong. What's right for one person can be wrong for another. I think everyone can live with this idea, because I am living with it. Someday, maybe, humanity will not be all that concerned about life styles, about the color of a person's skin, or about what God someone worships. We'll just try to live in harmony, letting other people live their life as best they can and find happiness where they can.

If homosexuality were taken for granted as much as heterosexuality is, there wouldn't be any problem. A lot of us think of homosexuality only in terms of sexual relations, but it's much more than that. My daughter is happy the way she is, and it is a whole way of life for her.

You know, anything that gays do sexually, heterosexuals also do. Sexual customs have changed in the last few years. It's more liberal now. There's a feeling that anything is acceptable between consenting, heterosexual adults. But when lesbians and gays do the same thing it is considered shocking, immoral, disgusting, and sinful.

Trying to Do Something About the Problem

Some parents develop a deep desire to fight back. They want to make life better for their own child and for all gays and lesbians. They are willing to take risks.

I don't have much to leave Betty. But I'm going to fight until my last breath to make it better for her. I want to get the laws changed. I want to change the political system. I may not be able to get anything done, but at least I'm going to try.

Chris suggested that we consider starting a parents' group. He thought it would be a good, interesting, and satisfying project for us. Jack and I agreed, and we contacted the Metropolitan Community Church. Slowly the group took shape, and we helped other parents.

About the time that Amy came out, the crisis hot line needed volunteers. I had just found out that Amy had considered killing herself. Volunteering for the hot line grabbed my attention because I thought, "Maybe I can help someone like Amy."

As it happened, after I completed my training my very first call was from a man who was gay. I think I was really able to help him. I took that call as a sign that I was supposed to do that work for awhile. And I did. I talked to many other gay people.

Setbacks

Sometimes when they least expected it, parents would find themselves falling back into old perceptions. It was disturbing, but it was only a temporary setback. What slowly came to consciousness was that they had experienced an inner change as they resolved the issues surrounding the setback. As parents began to investigate the sources of their reversals, they looked inside and saw that they were being controlled by old messages that no longer applied. The frightening thoughts were like holes in their thinking that they had to reweave with new information and new attitudes.

As a result, the entire fabric of their thinking became stronger. A new and surprising sense of freedom emerged. Parents frequently reported feeling more grown up and more in charge of their lives than ever before. They discussed these temporary setbacks in our interviews.

A boyhood friend of Mark's came by to return a tool he had borrowed. He asked me how Mark was doing. I knew he was aware that Mark is gay, but I found myself fumbling for words. After Dave left I felt like I had let Mark down. And I had.

I was feeling pretty good about Jane's being a lesbian when I picked up a pamphlet about lesbians. It said Jane had a choice. That pamphlet was written by someone who should know, and it really shook me. I wondered if Jane wanted to hurt me by choosing to be a lesbian. For a day or so I really thought she hated me and wanted to punish me by being gay. I was in a panic.

Then I talked to another mother who had had something like this happen to her. She told me how hard it was to find good information because few people have really researched why people are gay, but everybody had opinions about it. She said she'd just decided to pay attention to articles and books that made her feel better.

I thought that was a pretty good idea and decided to try it the next time. It took me a few days, but just talking with her had eased my scared and hurt feelings. I wish I knew for sure why Jane is gay, but I'm beginning to wonder if it is all that important after all.

The Light at the End of the Tunnel

Parents know the struggle will never really end because the reality of their lives and their children's lives is forever changing. But they are better prepared to face the future. They have grown to be more mature and less judgmental.

When my daughter was little, there were some things I was very moralistic about. I had some holier-than-thou attitudes. But now, after going through this experience of having a lesbian child, I have become more aware of what is going on. I'm not that judgmental of people anymore.

I think we're better people because of it. Our accepting it has helped our son reach his potential. He is not bothered with any aspect of being gay. And we're not either.

We have grown up as we examined our inner thoughts. It's almost indecent how much fun this has been.

Each step I took towards learning how to look at the homosexuality of my child left me stronger. I'm more certain of what I believe in, of what I consider important and of what I need. I feel more independent because I'm taking responsibility for myself. When I first found out I felt devastated. Now I feel tough.

chapter 6

Taking a Stand
and
Telling Others

Nobody must know—it's nobody's business but ours. What if the neighbors find out?

It would kill the grandparents. They're so old they couldn't possibly understand.

We don't talk about the sex life of our nongay children, so why should we talk about the sex life of our gay child?

Such comments and thoughts during early grief sent parents into a self-imposed prison of silence. Somehow we perceived that we and our children had broken a societal law. We saw ourselves as guilty of creating and being part of an unacceptable portion of society. There was no trial. Our guilt was self-judged, and we found that the prison door slammed shut with surprising speed and force. Opening that door and coming out was a long arduous process. It involved taking yet another risk. We had to go beyond changing our own inner views. To gain a new order of personal freedom, we had to take a stand against the prevailing views of this society.

We could not really accept our children without taking such a stand inwardly and, later, outwardly. Parents who love their children and yet try to appease society through elaborate secrecy usually do not find this fence-straddling at all satisfactory. It leaves the gay children feeling not understood, accepted or loved for what they truly are.

Words are the connecting link between our inner feelings and society. They teach us and control us. They taught us the old ways about homosexuality. But the power goes both ways. If we are to break out of our fear and silence, we have to risk uttering our own new words. They are the key to personal freedom. Without the telling, we can't have the freedom.

So, for parents, coming out and taking a stand involves verbally supporting a gay or lesbian child either directly or indirectly to someone else in society. This covers a wide variety of supportive statements and activities from disagreeing with negative comments to making television appearances. There are no hard and fast rules for what a parent should do to come out. Some parents work publicly while many others work on the grass roots one-to-one level. The common denominator is that in one way or another, parents speak out.

Whenever a parent is able to say, "I have a gay or lesbian child" to anyone outside the immediate family, there is an underlying message: "As his or her parent, whatever befalls my child befalls me. I will fight with and for my child, for we are intertwined in our history and in our love for each other. My child is not alone. I stand with him or her."

In various ways, parents recognized and expressed the significance of taking a stand in the following quotes:

The more I come out and the more I face my own feelings, revealing them to people I trust, the less depressed I am. I would say that now I have no depression about my daughter's being gay. I don't think any more, "Isn't it too bad?"

There is a strain in any relationship if one person has to cover up something that's important. In fact, it's deadly.

When other people say, "Why tell anyone?," they just don't understand. There's something about the telling process that makes you feel whole.

When my son first told me, I said, "I hope you're not going to tell anyone else." Then I began to realize that I couldn't impose that rule on him. We've all taught our children not to lie, yet we're tempted to say to our gay children, "Don't lie exactly, but live a lie."

We parents are a kind of bridge. We're a bridge between the closeted community and the larger community. Even though we're "tainted" by being associated with a stigmatized group, we're still a respected part of the larger, heterosexual majority.

The fact that we're risking "being tainted" or risking being identified with a stigmatized group gives us a certain kind of force that a group of, say, clergy might not have.

I don't always trust statistics, but I do believe that one out of every ten people is gay. When I'm in a group and they start talking negatively about gays, I'll say, "One out of every ten people is homosexual. Who is it in this group?" That usually shuts them up. It makes them think that they could be hurting someone unknowingly. They realize I'm not kidding. I don't like to shoot people down, but I would like them to regroup their thinking.

I think that those of us who are openly talking about gayness can give others a little courage to do it. We have found that once you start speaking out, it isn't bad at all. I was scared at first. I didn't know how people were going to react so I was very much on the defensive. I gave explanations on the latest research and so on. But now, if it comes up in conversation with somebody that I think really needs to know because I care about them or they care about me, I just tell them, period.

It is threatening to find ourselves, mild-mannered and law-abiding citizens, in a predicament involving conflicting values. Our dependency on society is usually subconscious until we have either broken or are unsure of the rules. We blame society, we submit to society, we love society, and we want to be an acceptable part of society. It is both "out there" and within us, contained in all our imprinted inner messages.

Taking a stand against society's injunctions is not to be taken lightly. In a sense, society understandably places pressure on us all to accept its rules of right and wrong. Through generations of experience, it has discovered many things that make human life good. Since we enjoy the benefits of society, it expects our allegiance. It offers painful penalties to nonconformers. But human life is not static. Change is necessary when new facts and situations call for a legitimate challenge to established ways.

Courage, self-awareness, and spirit are required of anyone who is challenging the status quo. When parents come out, we must first see society's disapproval as a condition somewhat of our own making. Only then can our inner belief system be questioned, clarified, and changed. Inner acceptance of gayness makes it easier to take a stand; and taking a stand causes us to feel acceptance at a gut level. We remain in self-imposed exile if we are so intimidated by fear of societal rejection that we stay ambivalent and silent.

The consequences of speaking up are usually less than we fear. When we come out of our suffocating cocoon of fear of "them" and what "they" think, we become our own persons. There is no greater prize we can win for ourselves.

Each time parents enter into a discussion with someone, somewhere, concerning homosexuality, we connect our inner feelings to someone else in the society. We in some way alter, both internally and externally, the prevailing prejudice. We often experience a sense of relief and it whets our desire to speak out again. We have a sense of being in close touch with reality, and we are reinforced by the knowledge that each revelation brings us closer to our children.

The simplicity of this idea disguises the difficulty of the action. Parents move in and out of being able to talk. Whom to tell, when to tell, if to tell, why and what to tell become daily questions. Each of us develops an individual style of coping. Psychological comfort increases and the telling is therapeutic whether or not those being told respond positively. The primary value of telling is in being real.

There are some wonderful parents who are totally out of the closet. I know one, and she says the first five years she didn't tell one soul. The last five years, she's been out everywhere. I think for most parents, it's been a step-by-step process.

I have found it such a good experience to tell people. Particularly for parents who are hurting I want to say "Tell the people you trust! It's wonderful for your mental health." But there are some who cannot bring themselves to tell a single person. As a result, it seems to eat them up because they are going on the assumption that the other person is going to disapprove. It's like living with that person's severe disapproval when you haven't yet received it. You've got all the torments of disapproval and rejection without ever having put it to the test. You have nothing to lose by telling, because you're already in misery.

And the fact is that 95 times out of 100, if you tell the people that you care about and who care about you, and tell them in a positive way, they are going to be not only supportive, but closer to you because you shared something important with them.

Fear can have tremendous power over us. We give that fear the power to control us. When parents build this up into a dreadful secret, it becomes something that has power over them. But once they confront it and talk about it, even if they get a bad reaction, which is unlikely, at least they feel they are being themselves.

It's such a good feeling to be yourself. Our children had the courage to be themselves, when they "came out" to us. And we should have courage too. It's a tremendous feeling. When you're being yourself, you don't have to account to anybody anymore. You're free.

Like children who test out their muscles and physical strength as their maturation develops, parents will come out when their emotional well-being is ready. We connect first with the people we feel safest with, then with people we are not so sure of.

Parents who stand against the common view did not just wake up one day and say, "I don't agree with these ideas. I will go out and speak for my child." When we chose to leave the cell of silence, we had to face that first "leap into decision," like the moment before deciding to make the first spring off the diving board. We recall the fear of the water, the urge to go to the edge, the retreat down the ladder, and finally the moment of taking the plunge. Either we go or we don't.

For parents of gays, those feelings are the same, but the movement is usually more cautious. First we jump in from the side of the pool, being careful to hold our nose. Only later do we jump from the lowest and then, it is to be hoped, the highest of the boards.

Standing against the prevailing view involves several stages of development:

–Facing our inner fear of going against society's homophobia.

–Openly acknowledging to a few trusted others that we are parents of gay people. (Some parents never feel a need to come out beyond this point.)

–Beginning to speak out in the public arena, in protected and friendly places.

–Telling potentially critical others who need to become educated.

–Engaging with other parents in public forums and media events where some in the audience are known to be unsympathetic or uninformed.

Slowly we began to tell a few people. We had told a minister. I had told a therapist. We had both talked to several people at the Metropolitan Church, and they were very understanding. They did not seem to be put off by my fears of what people would think. Then I told my brothers and sisters, and they all responded without any great surprise or shock. They were all supportive. Then I began to tell a few close friends. In all these cases, there was no bad reaction. In fact, I would say there was an improved feeling between myself and whoever I told. It was as if a barrier had come down.

In addition to the healthy need to be real, there are a variety of other motives for telling. We parents speak because we, too, feel the personal pain of being in a stigmatized minority, and we hate having to bear a penalty alone. We speak because we question the fairness of the stigma. We properly want justice for our children and ourselves. Finally we speak because we want to work to change the prejudice of society. We have learned that our negative inner messages are merely antiquated judgments based on a lack of truth. We have a deep desire to correct a misinformed society. This is how human society has been changed throughout history.

Dean, one of the men in my five-member carpool, is a good friend and has known about my son's gayness for several years. We were approaching my house on the Friday my wife and I were going to the second international convention of Parents FLAG when Dean said, "Well, Rod, have a good time in the Big Apple."

Someone else asked, "You're going to New York this weekend? What for?"

After a couple of seconds' hesitation, I said "Carolyn and I are going to a national convention of Parents and Friends of Lesbians and Gays. My oldest son is gay." I got out of the car immediately after that and nothing else was said, but I went to New York feeling like a million dollars. Since then I have told several people at work—making sure they know it's no secret. It won't be a problem anymore for me to talk about it, and I want you to know it's liberating. The sky didn't fall in, no friends dropped me, and as far as I can tell it hasn't changed a thing— except that now I don't have to keep quiet. I can make statements about the subject and give out information that people need to know. I recommend it highly. It only took me eight years.

I learned through my relationship with my daughter, that when you share some tough things together, it brings you closer. You know, we all go around with our protection, with our "onionskin" so people can't get near the part of us that's vulnerable. We don't want people to know too much about us for fear we'll get hurt.

When I got into the parents' group, a big "onionskin" came off. I found I could be my real self and talk freely, and say the things I couldn't yet say in other places. That's a big relief and is probably the main reason for the group's success. It provides a nurturing setting, so the therapeutic effects of telling and sharing can take place.

When we see the healing effects of revealing our real selves in a protected situation, we can then risk being real in an unprotected setting. And we find that that, too, is healing and validating, no matter how it turns out.

We parents erroneously think, "If I don't tell anyone, then no one will know." In fact, parents may be literally the last to know, because of their need to screen out what they perceive to be dangerous information.

How much better it is when we finally can say, "Yes, my child is gay. He or she came into the world with that destiny. There is no fault. I will not accept the prejudice."

When we keep the gayness of our son or daughter a big secret, we assume our friends or relatives haven't already figured it out for themselves. In fact they may know a lot and just aren't letting on.

I don't go around tapping people on the shoulder and saying, "I'm going to tell you something." Because it's nobody's business unless it is somebody who is important in our relationship, or unless I feel that telling will do some good. For example, I'm finding that I bring it up much more often if I feel that the conversation is moving to a point where negative comments are going to be made about minority groups, whether it be gays or women or different nationalities. This was a hard decision to make, but the more I talk about it, the easier it gets.

Frequently, it will come up if someone asks me what I'm doing that evening. And I'll say, "I'm going to a support group that I belong to. It's Parents and Friends of Lesbians and Gays. Gary is gay, you know." Then there may be a comment, like one of my friends who said, "Oh, I'm sorry." I said, "Well, what are you sorry about?" She replied, "Well, I just feel sorry for someone who will never have children, never have a happy life." Then I said, "Now you're doing what I did. You are projecting your idea of what happiness is onto somebody else. Gary is perfectly happy. So you don't have to feel sorry for him. I don't feel sorry for him. He's one of the happiest people I know." Her expression changed and she said, "I didn't know that."

I have many friends from church and most of them are pretty naive as to what gayness means. They desperately need to be educated, and I intend to do just that, but in a nonjudgmental way.

Most of the time, when parents reveal that their child is gay or lesbian, they are greeted with courtesy, warmth, and interest. Occasionally there is a sign of discomfort or the other person may change the subject.

Things are very similar when speaking before groups. We usually get great respect and courtesy from the audience. Occasionally, there may be a person present whose religion or background causes him or her to be hostile. When this happens, we listen carefully and then state that we do not pretend to have all the answers. But we don't back down.

There were a couple of people I told who didn't respond badly, but they kind of changed the subject as soon as they could. They weren't comfortable. I'm hoping they'll think about what I told them, but it's their problem. I intend to bring it up again because these people are relatives I see often.

Over the months, I've told more and more people. Jack and I have talked in front of many groups. The people seemed eager for information and tuned in to us in a healthy way. I felt very authentic and close to those people. It was almost a mystical experience for me. So, I've gotten a lot out of speaking, and I want to do more.

I decided it was time to branch out and tell a few more people. My brother is married to a woman who was rather forward-thinking and very broadminded, or so I thought. I told her about Don.

She said, "He isn't going to have surgery, is he?" This just threw me. She's a social worker with a degree, and she should know something about sexuality.

I said, "What do you mean?" Then she said, "Doesn't he want to be a woman?" She's always thought that gay men wanted to be women, and women wanted to be men. So I educated her. She really was totally ignorant.

Then I decided I'd tell my sister. Her remark was that it was all right with her and that she still wanted to be friends with Don as long as he didn't flaunt it. I asked her what she meant by that. And she said, "Well, act real prissy and all."

I said, "Has he ever before?" She admitted that he hadn't. I said, "I don't think he'll start doing it just because you know." Both these people have since come around to an accepting point of view.

There is an unspoken message conveyed when we speak for our gay children. It is that homosexuality doesn't need to be hidden or hushed up. Whether they know it or not, everyone has gay and lesbian relatives or friends within their family, business or friendship circles. Each time parents speak out, they're helping all these people.

Telling others brings homosexuality home to people. When we as parents talk about our own children, it reminds others of the gay people they may know. It is hard to hate someone you know and care for. It is even harder to permit the denial of civil rights to a member of your own family or friendship circle.

I think of things I've done that scared me but that lead to good feelings and growth. In the early years, I was nervous about going places where I would see and speak before large groups of gay people such as the Metropolitan Community Church or Dignity, the gay youth group. The culture says, "Don't get mixed up with gays." It implies, "You may be contaminated."

In actuality, I saw the people I met as being mirror images of my son and me. They showed appreciation, directly and indirectly, for our being there. We helped them with their parents, and they helped us understand our children. We came to admire them as human beings, and came to be outraged at the suffering they endured simply for being what they were: decent, responsible people who happened to belong to what society deemed an "out" group.

Parents can be held back by their own invisible nets of fear and oppression. Tuna fishermen report that dolphins are often accidentally trapped in the tuna nets. The dolphins could easily escape. The nets offer no real challenge to the dolphins' athletic abilities. But they become "frozen" and give up. These intelligent animals often die needlessly as they are pulled in with the tuna. I think parents kind of die inside when they can't get out of their own nets.

We long for society to change without our confrontation. But it doesn't work that way. The need for scapegoats and victims seems deep-rooted in those who have not faced their own submerged insecurities and resentments. We can have freedom for ourselves and our children only when we resolutely challenge oppressive bigotry. There is no substitute for courage and the will to act. Pastor Niemöller reminds us of what can happen if we wait for others to do the work.

> In Germany, the Nazis came for the Communists, and I didn't speak up because I wasn't a Communist. Then they came for the Jews, and I didn't speak up because I wasn't a Jew. Then they came for the trade unionists, and I didn't speak up because I wasn't a trade unionist. Then they came for the Catholics, and I didn't speak up because I was a Protestant. Then they came for me, and by that time no one was left to speak up.[1]

The decision to speak up is the measure of our commitment. Each time we tell another human being about having a gay or lesbian child, we take a step away from our own prejudice. A parent summarizes both the anxiety and satisfaction of learning to tell:

I started by telling people I felt sure of—people who would not reject me. These were people I trusted very much.

At first I told them only of my pain. I wanted to feel their sympathy. I didn't really care what they thought or believed. Gradually, as my outlook changed, I wanted to make sure they had their facts straight. I found many of them had incorrect information, as I once had, so then my goal became to educate them and change their view.

Each time I told someone, I felt queasy, unsure, and frightened beforehand because I didn't know what reaction I was going to get.

Each time I felt much better afterward, whether the reaction was whole-hearted support, which it often was, or an uncomfortable changing of the subject. I think every act of telling develops confidence even if it's at the elementary level of asking for sympathy.

In spite of considering myself out of the closet, and being proud of that fact, I still find myself in certain situations where I feel the desire to hide the fact that I have a gay child. This feeling always surprises me. The way I have handled this is to acknowledge that I still have some feelings I'm not proud of—feelings of homophobia. So the next time I'm in a similar situation, if I am able to speak up, to tell about my daughter in a positive way, in a way that is filled with pride in her, then I am really exhilarated.

I had been for so long controlled by what I thought other people's opinions were, that I found it incredibly freeing to act on what my opinion was. Actually, I never had a bad experience from the people I told, and now, if I did, it wouldn't bother me much.

Having felt, even a few times, the freedom of moving away from damaging conformity, I started taking some public actions. Today, I am more and more openly political.

I now appear on television and radio. I make public speeches for gay rights and have my picture in the paper. I will not tolerate any negative comments against gay people in my presence. I feel anger and real disgust at homophobic statements and jokes, even though I myself sat in helpless silence only a few years ago.

Maybe it sounds saccharin, but I feel it's a real privilege to fight for something I believe in. I'm in it for myself too, you know, not just for others. All of us will have a better life when we don't have to put any group down in order to feel okay about ourselves. If parents don't speak out, then they're part of the problem. Maybe that's too judgmental. Let's say I want parents to progress to the point where they'll be able to speak openly about their own child and for the rights of all gay persons. It takes a long time to get to this point. It isn't easy to get there. Many parents don't get that far, but they continue to grow. Once you're in this thing, there's no end to your growing.

Some parents may not be political, but they are supportive and do a lot of good in a quiet way. If every gay person in our society felt accepted by his or her parents, there would be no "gay problem." Parents shouldn't feel bad if they go only as far as accepting their own child. They've had to change to get to that point. The door is open for movement that can come about later with changing circumstances.

NOTE FOR CHAPTER 6

[1]John Bartlett, *Familiar Quotations* (Boston: Little, Brown and Co., 1980), p. 824.

chapter *7*

The Rest
of the Family

*I have no qualms about accepting my son. I love him as much as
ever. But now my husband and I are in the closet. We cannot share this
with our families. If we were invited to my only brother's house, and my
son wanted to bring his friend, whatever would I say?*

Whether they are explicitly told about it or not, the
grandparents, siblings, aunts and uncles, in-laws and cousins,
will all be affected directly or indirectly by the gayness of a
family member. Those who know will have to explore their
values, their fears, their commitment. Those who don't know
are apt to sense a barrier, an unhappy change in family
dynamics; this will undoubtedly be disturbing to them.

The choice whether to tell the rest of the family is usually
placed on the shoulders of the parents. No matter which choice
they make there will be pain. They can withdraw from their
extended families into pain and isolation, or they can open up
their pain and consider new possibilities. In our contact with
parents, and in our interviews, we have seen these two basic

reactions, even though they come disguised in fifty-seven varieties.

Parents gave a great deal of energy and thought to other family members. Over and over, parents wrestled with questions about their families. They were concerned about how everyone would view them as parents. And they were concerned about any adverse effect the news would have on individual members.

The wide range of responses that came out in our interviews touched a variety of personal and family situations. These taught us that no parent is alone in his or her reaction. Also, by getting in touch with a range of reactions we can see the struggles within the family with more compassion.

Some of our married respondents shared information about how their marriage itself was affected. There were also discussions about the pros and cons of telling grandparents, siblings, aunts, and uncles. Parents shared how they handled the incorporation of the gay child's lover into the family. A gay man talked about some basic assumptions that have to be examined before families can come to terms with their homophobic feelings. And fortunately, we were able to interview several siblings of the gay children. These siblings gave us a good picture of the seesaw effect, the early pulling apart and then drawing together that was typical of so many accepting families.

EFFECT ON THE MARRIAGE

In the case of married parents, our interviews showed that the marriage itself was affected when the couple faced the fact of having a gay child. As each person felt his or her grief, change and tension occurred within the relationship. Some couples reported feeling more united as they joined together in shaking old beliefs. But the more prevalent reaction was a kind of separateness during the initial mourning period. Each person felt alone as old frictions were aggravated and new ones added.

With time, however, the couple settled into a day-by-day adjustment to their grief. Their pain lost some of its intensity, and they began to turn again towards each other. When one spouse made a move towards acceptance, he or she was often able to help the other make the same move.

Ruth and I have had some uncomfortable discussions about Debby's gayness. Ruth needs to talk about things that are bothering her. I tend to "clam up" and try to reason things out within myself rather than discuss them openly. This has created problems. And because we first thought parents were the cause, we spent a lot of time blaming ourselves and each other. We hurt one another over this.

Sometimes I feel bad about my relationship with my husband. I'm not comfortable talking to him about Mary so we don't talk about it much. He thinks there's nothing to talk about. She's gay. That's it. There's nothing he can do. He'll continue loving her and seeing her during holidays and whenever. But he'll never mention it to her. Those are his wishes. I know it's painful for him, so his way of handling it is to ignore it. I think he'd probably burst into tears if we ever got into a deep discussion about Mary's being gay. But I don't want to handle it the way he does. Sometimes I feel pulled apart by this.

I realize we used the fact that Carrie is a homosexual as an excuse for not dealing with some of our other problems. Outwardly we seemed to be fighting over how to handle Carrie's gayness; but in truth we were having fights over things that didn't have anything to do with Carrie. For instance, the problems married people have when children leave home, the so-called empty nest syndrome. We were going through that when Carrie told us she was gay. We let Carrie's situation keep us from dealing with the sadness and grief that we were feeling about the loss of our parent role, the mom-and-dad role. I think it took us longer to be able to understand that loss, because we thought this gayness was the source of all our difficulties.

It's interesting that finding out Hal was gay didn't cause marital troubles for us. I think for most parents it does. It's a problem they don't need. We weren't getting along all that well, and we didn't need it

either. We were both reared in troubled times and in troubled families.
We both had the trappings of being well-adjusted, but when it came to
living with someone else and nurturing that other spouse, we didn't
have it.

So it was strange that learning about Hal's being gay didn't create
a lot of problems with our relationship. Considering our lack of
information and our need to present a good front, it should have.
Somehow it seemed clear what we should do. Whereas we didn't always
understand our own relationship, with this issue we understood each
other. We knew we had to work on supporting each other and
supporting Hal. We went in that direction. As each month passed, we
handled it better and better.

I don't think we ever had quarrels over it. Oh, maybe some
competition. Bob or I might say, "Well, I'm moving along with it a little
faster than you." By and large we held together very well.

OTHER CHILDREN IN THE FAMILY

The people we interviewed had strong nuclear family
relationships, whether they were married or not. They often
spoke of the other members of the immediate family and how
they were affected. We were impressed by certain elements of
the interactions within the families. There were family rules,
but the rules were flexible. Anger and disappointment were
freely expressed, and individuality was accepted as the norm.
Family pride, respect, and closeness were typical. In our talks
with other gays and lesbians, many were not as fortunate as the
gay children in these accepting families.

Most of our parents told their other children as soon as
possible, since they knew that secrets were barriers to familial
support and understanding. They felt their gay child deserved
and needed the support of the family circle, and their other
children needed to know what was going on. Very young
children were not told until it was felt they could understand.

The children were torn by a mixture of feelings. Some
teenage siblings were exposed to fierce inner pressures—"Will
my brother's being gay somehow rub off on me? Will they think

I'm a lesbian?" Caught in their own personal crisis, they were unable to offer much support.

On the other hand, many older siblings tended to play a helpful role. Often, these older siblings were the first to know and acted as understanding intermediaries between the parents and the gay member. A good rule of thumb seems to be: If the gay child's siblings got along well with him or her before the coming out, they will usually continue to do so afterwards. If the relationships were never close, or were strained, coming out can become another bone of contention. In other words, the initial reactions will be affected by factors such as the age of the children, family traditions, and the nature of the relationships in each family.

Parents recalled how their other children reacted:

My gay son, Gary, is very close to his older brother Pete, who is twenty months older. Pete has always taken care of Gary. They were together constantly. I didn't know how Pete would react. He's not macho, but he's associated with a lot of fellows who are. While he's very loving, sweet and compassionate, I'd say Pete was always much more into sports and athletics and all the stereotypical things that males do.

After things settled down a bit, I got a chance to talk to Pete about his reaction. He said, "I have no problem with that at all. I love Gary more than any person in the world. He's still Gary—he's still my brother."

Then he said something that showed me I had an irritated older son who was really hurt that we would even for a moment question how he would react. He said, "I do get tired of people always wanting to know how I'm going to handle Gary's gayness. Dad, how did you think I was going to react? What do you think of me? How could you think I would hurt my own brother!"

Our other children had no problem accepting the fact that Rich is gay. The news was no "big deal," and they are all comfortable with it now. One of our sons was a worry for us. Eric is the macho type and had made some derogatory remarks at times about gays. When Rich told him, Eric was very accepting. It didn't bother him at all, and he's been great about it ever since. So, our worries were pointless. I think it speaks for the maturity and the close family feeling that the children have for each other. Nothing is going to break that up!

Andy came out to his married sister before he told me. Even though she was very accepting and her attitude was good, my daughter was under a strain until I found out too. But she was very helpful in her responses to him. Once when he was upset because he hadn't found a special person she said, "Andy, you can't look for a person so intensely. It's like trying to catch a butterfly. If you're watching it'll never happen. But if you're not, the butterfly might sit on your shoulder." After that he didn't seem to have that feeling of urgency and was more satisfied.

THE SIBLINGS SPEAK

The observations just presented were accounts by parents as to how they saw their other children responding. Now we want to present some accounts, at greater length, by the sisters and brothers themselves. All of the incidents, except the first one, involve siblings who were in their early teen years when they found out.

As we listened to these and other children in our families, we noticed some common initial reactions:

–Older siblings (past their teen years) who were secure in their sexual identity had fewer problems with the news. Those who had the experience of having gay and lesbian friends were able to see the situation in terms of the larger social issues.

–Some siblings who found out during their stressful teen years expressed a feeling that the gay child was responsible for shattering the image of a "perfect" family.

–Teenagers may also have felt a loss of parental support when their parents were in the early stages of their own grief.

–Some youngsters feared being verbally (or even physically) attacked by their peers.

–For many teenagers, learning of the sibling's gayness triggered questions about their own sexuality. Fearing and questioning their own sexuality is a very common occurrence for young people as well as for their parents. It is a threat because in the early stages they see gayness as a handicap at best, and as an affliction at worst.

All of these reactions and feelings were worked through as the teens underwent a learning process remarkably similar to their parents.

Valerie

Valerie was in her middle twenties when her younger brother came out to her. Her age and wide range of experiences were major factors in her early and total acceptance of her brother's gayness. She is a person who sees the political aspects of our society's anti-gay attitudes.

For me it wasn't hard when Chris came out, because a lot of my friends have been lesbians and gay men. I feel really positive about people who are gay or lesbian. The sickness or health of a relationship has to be judged by what is going on between the two people. I judge a couple by whether there is mutual respect and whether the people are growing in the same direction. It's also important whether a relationship helps people take responsibility for what's going on in society or whether it's just a nice comfy place that helps people not deal with society's problems.

For many of the women I know, coming out was a positive thing. These couples seemed to care more about each other and were more open with each other than most heterosexual couples. They weren't worried about looks or power or whatever. That made a lot of sense to me. My experiences with the gay men and lesbians I know have made me question society's anti-gayness and the thinking that there's something wrong or sick about loving someone of the same sex.

Valerie then talked about what she saw as the source of much parental misinformation and guilt. Her awareness showed an ability to empathize with the feelings and needs of others.

One day I was in a grocery store line and picked up a woman's magazine that offered advice to parents of gays. It criticized parents by repeating the classic stereotyped thinking that distant fathers and domineering mothers produce sick children. People who get their information from articles like that would, of course, be very upset by their child's gayness. Reading such articles, it's no wonder that parents feel something is dreadfully wrong and that it's all their fault.

For many gay people and their parents it's a process of groping past all the anti-gayness that's around. Gay men and lesbian women have to affirm what they naturally want to do, or what they've decided to do, depending on the person.

She discussed ideas that might help parents come to terms with their grief and closed her interview with a hope for the future.

I've seen my mom and dad struggle with letting all of us live our own lives. They know their children aren't six years old anymore and are going to follow their own paths. I believe it would help all parents to keep this idea as their bottom line and to remind themselves of that often. No amount of fretting will change it.

I think it's important for parents to understand how much of their disappointment about their child's coming out is due to the anti-gay propaganda that we're flooded with, and how much of their disappointment might also come from wanting to relive their own lives through their child. It seems to me that a lot of parents want their child to have a wedding just so they can share that experience with their friends. For awhile my parents wanted that too. But they reconsidered and decided they wanted a more real and honest relationship with their friends. I remember their saying, "Well, those friends who are truly close will know and understand. Those who are judgmental and anti-gay don't matter to us anyway. So, too bad for them." This sort of thinking would help all parents.

You know, everybody concerned would be helped if society could begin to understand why it is so anti-gay. If everyone could view homosexual relationships with a more open mind, the stigma attached to being gay would be reduced. The gay movement has begun to spread this idea among people. It's a little like the way the women's movement spread the idea among millions of people that women should be respected and shouldn't have to accept a secondary position. The whole society will be better as women are appreciated and as gay people are appreciated.

Susan

Susan was a junior in high school when her brother, six years her senior, told her he was gay. She felt torn to some extent by the news. But by examining her innermost perceptions, she was able to resolve her conflict. As she became more independent, she became a quiet champion of her family's effort to improve society's image about gayness.

After my brother told me he was gay, I had feelings of disappointment that he wasn't an "ideal" brother. I think that was caused partly by my own desire to be "ideal," sort of perfect. If he wasn't perfect it really affected my feelings about whether I was okay or not. I asked myself, "Could I be gay, too?"

Knowing about Chris made me in some ways more willing to deal with people who I knew were gay. Before, I probably would have just shut them out. Beyond that, I don't really think the fact that he was gay affected me. It didn't make me feel that the family was weird. In fact, I felt good about the way we handled it, when we finally got around to talking about it. I think I was probably too caught up in my own life, trying to be more independent and that kind of thing, to focus on my brother's gayness. It wasn't as much of an upheaval for me as it was for my parents. In some ways I think it was good because it made us talk about things that we really hadn't talked about before.

Susan was candid in discussing her occasional wish for the problem not to "be." We were glad that she brought it up. It is a wish that is almost universal in families when the members are faced with tough problems.

There have been times when I have wished Chris weren't gay. Sometimes I have feelings of wanting the family to be more average.

Like when we get together with the cousins, and they talk about their engagements and having children, and so forth. There's a part of that that is really appealing. So sometimes I do want that. I want something that's a little bit closer to average.

But I don't think it's his being gay that bothers me as much as some elements of his personality. In other words, I have issues with him that are not centered around gayness.

She showed concern about taking or not taking a stand for gays and lesbians.

I don't feel free to talk about my brother. Partly it's because I was never quite sure how Chris felt about my just coming right out and saying, "Yes, my brother's gay." Especially when I am with people who might know him. Several years ago I mentioned it to some people who knew him and he told me, "I prefer that you not say that." So I stopped telling anyone except close friends about it. But now it seems like I am basically open with people who will be respectful of the information. I might mention it to them, if it comes up.

There have been times when I've said, "I don't like gay jokes," or "I don't like your saying that." I'm more willing to stand up for gay people, and I think that's good. Every once in a while if someone jokes about gays, and I think that person is receptive, I'll say, "Well, my brother is gay and I love him, so if you make fun of gay people, you're making fun of somebody I care about. I don't like that and I don't think you would either if you were in my place." Then sometimes I'll tell them all about it. But I don't really make a big cause out of it.

Denny

Denny was fifteen years old when he found out for sure that his brother, Craig, was gay. He was struggling with all the usual developmental problems of a boy his age and then had to suffer through what most people in the immediate families of gays and lesbians fear will happen but usually doesn't. He endured open and hard ridicule from his peers and suffered a loss of status. Even so, he made significant changes in his attitude toward gay people and continues to do so. The brothers are now close friends, and Craig was best man at

Denny's wedding. At the time of our interview, Denny was twenty-two.

I had heard some kidding about Craig's being gay from a guy in the band, but I was still pretty shocked and surprised when Craig told us. I was upset, you know, sort of grieving. It seemed like there was an end to my idea of what "normal" is. I had thought that our whole family was perfectly normal, but Craig's being gay was abnormal. To me the norm is straight.

At school I was treated like I was gay too. The kids would holler that Craig and I were both fags. They would do that on the bus or at band practice—any public place where they thought they could ridicule me. One day I just got fed up with it and hit one of them. That stopped him and the other nasty kids as well.

There was another reason why they shut up too. I was going wild with women then. It was a good move for me to show how heterosexual I was for awhile. It was the logical thing to do. The next year, after Craig graduated, the whole thing died down.

In the next section, there is searching for the reason for the homophobia that hurt him.

People act terrible when they're stupid and ignorant and afraid. And the kids in my class were stupid and ignorant and afraid about homosexuality. It's the guys that will give you trouble. They all called each other queer. The guys were very afraid they could turn into homosexuals. Except me. I really don't have any homosexual tendencies. I've always been fascinated by females. I've never had the problem of being worried about being gay.

The problems that Denny had at school were not his only concerns about his brother's gayness.

You have a crisis when your idea of what the world is doesn't fit what it actually is. The closer you are to the part that doesn't fit, the more of a shock it will be. You have a family crisis when someone is not what you thought they were.

Craig's a smart guy, and he's strong. He's my older brother, and everything he does has meaning to me. His being gay just wasn't in my picture of him. You know, it threatens your entire system when something like this happens. It threatens your whole belief in the world. You're not sure of anything. When things aren't what they seem, it's a big shock.

I had to deal with my feelings about my brother. He does not look at girls in the same way that I look at girls. I would rather that he had been more like me—that we could have done some stuff together. I lost any chance of searching for girls with my brother, which would have been fun. Since we weren't the same, that was something I missed out on.

Denny talked about the rest of his family members. Even with the pain he was subjected to by insensitive peers, he made a significant adjustment.

Mom and Dad cried a lot, yelled a lot, and went to group meetings. Dad moped around. Both of them spent a lot of time blaming themselves. They didn't pay much attention to me. For a while there it seemed like I lost them.

Still, we all accepted Craig's being gay instead of hoping he would change. We didn't hide anything about it from ourselves. Mom and Dad had made sure that we all knew, and I think that was a good idea.

I didn't help Craig much at first. I was too busy coping with it myself. I wasn't ready to help him. I was only fifteen. It's not realistic to expect someone of that age to do much. Craig talked to me some and asked me how I was doing. When he did that, I did try to reassure him. As time went on, I felt better and wanted to understand him. He was different even when he and I were growing up. He didn't like to play sports, and he didn't go outside for recess. And he never said he didn't like girls. I think that was because girls just never were that important to him.

I would change Craig if I could, as I believe he would change himself. I don't want either of us to hurt anymore. But I certainly wouldn't want to change all gays. In reality being gay is not a problem except for how we cope with it. Gays are just another group of interesting people. They have a different perspective on life. Gays don't make me nervous the slightest bit.

Jane

Jane, Denny and Craig's sister, was thirteen when she received the news that her oldest brother was gay. She is the youngest and only daughter in her family. Her early experience after Craig came out was different from Denny's, but nevertheless there was a period of adjustment for her. Jane, who was nineteen when we interviewed her, began her discussion of how the news affected her with the usual "finding out."

Craig called a family conference to tell us about his being gay. But I didn't realize what it meant. I had no idea how bad it was on Craig or Mom and Dad. The only bad effect it had on me directly was that it made me scared that I might be gay also. I worried about that off and on for months—really until I had sex with a boy and found out how much I liked it. (She laughs.) I don't want my dad to hear this.

Jane's school experience was less dramatic than her brother's. However it was not without problems.

I didn't have trouble at school the way Denny did. In fact, for a long time I didn't even know how badly Denny was being hassled. The kids who were bothering Denny were being nice to me. I never have figured out why they were nice to me, but mean to him. It was kind of odd. But after I found out I went to war with them. Nobody is going to say anything about my brothers and get by with it.

I had a chemistry teacher who was always making comments in class about "fags and queers." That was hard to take. But I tried to consider the source. She was also very seductive with the fourteen-year-old boys in the class. If she had been more intelligent and nicer it would have been harder to deal with her stupidity, but she wasn't a wonderful person. So it was easy for me to just hate her.

I was pretty emotional about the school thing for a while, and I turned into a self-righteous liberal. For a long time I was furious about the way people feel about homosexuality. Then I realized that they are ignorant about it, the way I used to be—just totally ignorant.

The effects on the family life are sometimes dramatic. Jane found a near reversal of roles as she comforted the other family members.

I didn't go around thinking everything was hunky-dory about my family like I had before. Everyone was unhappy, and that made it hard to deal with. We were still close. We still cared. But people weren't as much fun. More than one of us was unhappy at any given time. There were outbursts, and I would try to get people to feel better.

I was sometimes impatient about my parents' blaming themselves. I wished they would just accept it and go on with their lives. It was hard for me to know what to say or to understand everything they were feeling. But everyone was hurting, and I tried to help by listening and reassuring.

I never wished that Craig weren't gay. I think he's just fine like he is—except that he does overspend. He'll do well at a job with no problems at all. I sometimes worry about his having sex with too many people. I'm afraid he could get venereal disease or worse.

For a while he had a lover, a partner. I spent time with them. It was just a relationship to me. At first, seeing them hug was kind of hard. But not for long. You can't hate love between two people. His love affair made me feel good. He was happy. I guess if you're worried about your own sexuality you might hate to see two males or two females touching in a sexual way. If you're sure of your own sexuality and you see it over a period of time, it becomes a normal thing.

Craig and his lover were a part of our family. When they broke up, I felt like I would if anyone I cared about got a divorce. I hurt for Craig, because I knew he was going through a hard time. I felt sad for him. I didn't think they'd ever break up. I felt we'd lost a family member, and I still really and truly like his ex-lover—a lot.

For Craig, being gay is a very deep thing. I know that to come out and say he was homosexual was the single hardest thing he's ever done. He told me about it. But homosexuality is right for him. He had to be who he is. I'm glad he told all of us.

I've learned a lot from all of this. Having a gay brother opened my mind to other people. I even understand conservatives better. I'm more tolerant.

As a family we hung in there. We didn't deny any part of our feelings. We didn't pretend we weren't hurting when we were. I believe you'll hurt the gay person a lot more if you don't face up to how you really feel. It may take years to learn and accept and to understand, but once you get there, it's worth it.

TELLING THE GRANDPARENTS

Bringing their own parents the news was one of the hardest tasks for parents. Parents viewed the grandparents as being vulnerable: "With their health problems, I just wouldn't want them to hear about this on top of everything else." Or as uninformed: "They are of a different generation, and they just couldn't understand or handle it." Or as possibly rejecting: "I wouldn't want my gay son or lesbian daughter to be looked on as an unacceptable person by his or her own grandparents."

As parents began to understand their own homophobia and worked at getting rid of it, the power of their reasons for not sharing with their parents dimmed. Many chose to include the grandparents in their family situation. A few parents let their parents know early in their grieving time, but on the whole this was not the case.

The grandparents who were told handled the information well. Though their knowledge about gayness was limited, they certainly knew what it was. The relationship between the grandparents and their children and grandchildren took on a renewed sense of togetherness. Their biological bond was fortified as they worked to understand what was happening.

Telling a Grandfather

My father was eighty-one years old when I told him about Bill. It had been worrying me for several years, and I finally told him. I guess I never would have if it had been easy not to. What I mean by that is that given the choice, I don't stick my neck out. I take the easy route. I avoid any controversy. But I have trouble telling lies. I have always prided myself on being honest, even if it made me look bad. Sometimes I think I go overboard. Anyway, it seems that when I can't be honest with people who mean something to me, a barrier goes up between them and me. I was beginning to dread seeing him because I couldn't be myself with him.

So I told him. And he said, "I'm glad you didn't tell your mother." I told him that I was sorry I hadn't because it had affected our relationship. I wasn't being honest with her about something that was extremely important to me. At least if I had told her, we would have understood each other better.

After he had some time to digest it, my dad began to talk more reasonably about it. I gave him some of the literature from our parents' group, and he read it.

Overall I think he took it pretty well. He still asks about Bill and when he talked to him on the phone he invited Bill to come and live with him if he got a job in his town. And whether he takes it well or not, I have it off my chest. It's my son and he's my father. We all need to be honest with each other. I felt closer to my dad after our talk, and he seemed to feel closer to me.

Telling a Grandmother

My seventy-four-year-old mother was planning to visit for three weeks last month. She didn't know about her grandson's homosexuality or about our involvement in Parents FLAG. My wife and I decided to avoid raising the possibility that this visit would be the time of her enlightenment. That meant writing to a few people to remove "Parents of Gays" from their mailing envelopes to our home (since we are both employed outside the home), not being able to answer the hot line, and telling a few folks that when they called we might not be able to talk freely. It also meant boxing up all the materials, books, pamphlets, and newsletters that cluttered my study.

We went to this extent—not because we are ashamed of our son or unwilling to discuss the matter with my mother—but because we had promised Michael that this topic was to be raised with family members at his initiative and on his terms. In fact, during the past four and one half years there have been many times when I've wanted to be more open and honest with my mother. On the one hand I had the feeling that she would understand, that her love for her grandson and our family could sustain her through any family crisis. But—to be perfectly honest—there was that nagging doubt: What if she finds out and rejects our wonderful son? Over the years, then, our visits with her have always created this mental game of ping-pong for me.

Before Mother's arrival I said to my wife, "There's one letter addressed to 'Parents of Gays' that comes into the house two or three times a year that I can't change. The Internal Revenue Service will not send their tax exemption correspondence to a post office box; they send it only to a person's home. We'll just have to take that chance. If it comes in, and she asks about it, we'll tell the truth and take it from there."

Things went well for two weeks. My anxiety level lessened with each passing day. One day I came home from work to find the mail stacked on the kitchen counter—and the IRS letter was on top. My heart raced. From the living room I heard, "Tom, there's a letter that came in today that raises questions. Will you tell me about it and tell me the truth?" Her tone was soft, yet firm; one that I have known for almost fifty years. "Well, Mother," I said, "Sue and I are members of a wonderful group of parents who love and support their homosexual children. You have a gay grandson."

I sat down, and we talked for about two hours. It was evident that she was willing to try to understand. She asked many questions. I had so much to tell her that at times it just poured out. We agreed that in the remaining week of her visit she'd do some reading and we'd do more talking together. All this was so new to her.

As we talked I began to realize that she hadn't said she still loved her grandson. I've always expected too much too soon from my parents. I needed to hear those words now. When they didn't come fast enough I began to choke up. With tears in my eyes I blurted out, "Mother, it will be like putting a knife in my heart if you reject Michael. We love him so much." She reached over to hold my hand and assured me that she would never turn her back on him.

A little later we went to pick up Sue from work. When she got into the car, I told her that the IRS letter had arrived that afternoon. There was silence. "It's all right," Mother said. "There's no tragedy where there's love."

Aunts and Uncles

Where the immediate family is concerned, it is just about inevitable that some facing up to the issue will have to take place. But where other relatives are concerned, a different decision must be made. The generations that some of these relatives came from were exposed to much homophobia, so it is natural to have some reservations about telling them.

As parents and individuals we have ties and ego involvement with them. We were expected to accomplish in ways that would shed credit on the larger family. We have old rivalries with our brothers, sisters, and cousins. Will they consider us failures if we tell them about our gay child? Did we disgrace them? Will it cause serious upset, or worse? Will we be distanced? How will our gay child and his or her lover be received? What about the holidays?

At first glance, one might assume that our close relatives—our own parents, sisters, brothers, and cousins—would be a source of nurture. The blunt truth is, we can't count on it. Once again we confront the old questions. Should we stay in the closet? At what price—to ourselves, our child, and our immediate family?

Our general experience is that there is health and healing in telling the truth. But there can be exceptions. There is no substitute for trusting one's intuitions.

One parent told his sister, and six months later found out his sister also had a lesbian daughter:

After we found out, I told my sister within a few months. I told her we were struggling with it, but that we were making progress. She was completely supportive. A few months later, one of her own daughters told her that she was lesbian. The fact that I had talked to her about Anne had been a big help to her. When she got the news, she knew she wasn't alone.

At some point, I decided to write my sister and her husband that Jeannie was lesbian. I received a nice letter back saying they understood and that they had some gay acquaintances they liked. Later we went up to visit them for a weekend. In talking about our families we mentioned Jeannie, and my sister said, "Why do you need to tell anyone?" Not the most awful remark but somehow I felt from this and her other comments that she was disapproving. I know she is conservative on a lot of things, and I read into her remark that gayness would be better off not mentioned.

In letters I have written them since, I mention Jeannie and gay matters, but they don't respond to these topics. The truth is, our relationship was distant before Jeannie's lesbianism came up. It still is. Yet, I don't think telling hurt the relationship. It may even have helped it a little in other ways.

Sometimes a relative just "clams up," but later moves to a more open position. It may take them time to adjust just as it does parents.

Fairly soon after Sam told us, I decided to tell my brother. He is a warm, caring person and was close to Sam all the while he was growing up. He accepted the news easily. He sensed my pain and felt sympathy for the adjustment we had to make.

My wife and I would occasionally talk about Sam and his lover or mention gay issues or events. I noticed my sister-in-law never said anything in response. She is from a conservative religious tradition that might make homosexuality a forbidden subject, so I assumed she was uncomfortable with it and disapproving.

We decided to continue to mention the topic anyway. We did so casually but repeatedly over a period of years with the pattern remaining about the same. One of the nicest surprises I have had grew out of this situation. We had a special guest speaker at one of our parents' meetings. I invited my brother and when he arrived for the meeting, his wife was with him. She took part in the rap groups and took an active, friendly role in interacting with both the parents and gay people there. She talked about how proud she was of her lesbian niece. I was really grateful for the caring she showed and respected her making the decision to come.

A moral I drew from this: "Be careful about giving up on anyone's capacity to change." I know one result—it opened positive new feelings towards her for me, and strengthened good feelings about the family.

Another parent described why she has chosen not to tell her own siblings.

I have not told members of my family such as my brothers and sisters. I've thought about it, and I'm still not telling them. I don't see them as being very open. I think I could tell at least one brother. I probably could tell all of them if I wanted to, but I still don't want to.

I think the people in our generation, people who are now in their fifties, sixties, and seventies, have a harder time than people in their thirties or forties. Many in our generation were taught that homosexuality, even divorce, and a lot of other customs were sinful and immoral. They have a very hard time changing their outlook. Come to think of it I don't remember homosexuality being talked about in my background. I never heard my mother or father ever mention it. They had other things to worry about during the depression. As far as homosexuality was concerned I was just totally unaware, and so were my brothers and sisters. I wasn't even very familiar with the word. I think I was well along in years before I knew there was such a thing.

Some of our parents found an enormous amount of help when they told their own sisters and brothers. The next quote is a good example of this.

The smartest thing I ever did was to tell my sister right away. Martha was there for all of us in every way. She knew about homosexuality, and she knew about feelings. She helped us sort through whatever was bothering us. When the children were confused and acting up, she was able to explain how they were feeling. There was a time when everyone in the family went off into separate corners. But she kind of grabbed hold of each of us and brought us back together. I don't think we'd have done nearly as well without her.

THE LOVERS

On the obstacle course towards acceptance, one of the hurdles is what to do about the lovers. Even though gay people may often use the word "partner," the parents' ears hear "lover." To parents, the word "lover" is prickly in itself. Its connotations are associated with the ideal of youthful, heterosexual romance. "Lover" goes with moon, spoon, June, bridal gown, and babies. "Lover" may also suggest illicit love. Long after parents have made peace with the reality of gayness, and even with the partner of the gay child, many still have trouble saying the word "lover."

The truth is that we are dealing here with deep areas of parental resistance and residual homophobia. While we are undergoing all kinds of changes about our child's being gay, there rides along in some inner place a hope—a hope that maybe some miracle will happen and somehow our child will cease being gay. Acknowledging the sexual aspect of our child's life and knowing his or her lover causes that old unrealistic hope to fade rapidly.

Those of us who are fortunate enough to meet and get to know our child's lover generally report this as being a very positive experience. When we meet the lesbian or gay lover, and see how satisfying and happy is their relationship, we realize our child is not alone. We realize our child is not the only fine gay person in the world.

The first time John brought his lover home there was an uneasiness for me, because I was worried that I might make him feel uncomfortable. It wasn't that I didn't want him to visit, or that I couldn't accept him. That didn't enter into it. I was fearful that I might make some statement very unintentionally that would make him feel unwelcome. But after the first time, there's been no problem at all.

Shortly after Amy told us, she invited her lesbian lover, Peggy, to come over. Even though she had been in our house many times before and knew we liked her, Peggy was obviously uneasy now that we knew she was a lesbian and our daughter's lover. We could see she was nervous. So when she came in, we hugged her, and said, "Don't you worry for a moment over how we feel about you—we love you just like we did before." Peggy said she felt better and that she had been afraid we would hold her somehow responsible for Amy's being a lesbian. I don't know all that much about Amy's relationships, but as far as I know, this was Amy's first love affair with a girl. This friend had recognized her homosexuality several years before Amy had recognized her own, so she was afraid Amy's parents might say, "Well, you caused it." We assured her, "No, neither of us thinks that at all. Amy is still an individual and could have said 'No' if she didn't feel that way towards you."

On the question of "Where will they sleep?" we personally lean toward the position that our children at some point in their maturity become guests in our house. We have the right to state the ground rules of our piece of turf—for the nongay children or the gay children. And we have the right to let the rules bend and evolve as the relationships evolve.

I know people differ on this matter because of religious traditions, or the way they were brought up. For ourselves, we give priority to fairness. We had to adjust to our heterosexual kids having "live-in" arrangements. We finally came around to letting them share a bedroom in our house. Fairness says the same principle should apply to our gay child and her lover.

I'm at the point in my acceptance where homosexuality has very little, if any, negative connotation to me. The sex idea has ceased to bother me. Somewhere along the line, I lost that. Pretty soon after our son formed that relationship with Marty, my uneasiness left. That relationship plus more knowledge helped. The more knowledge I gained, the easier I felt.

What did hurt us was when George and Marty broke up. Marty had become a familiar figure in our home. I had genuine, deep affection for him. When they decided to part, I had the feelings parents must have when one of their married children decides to divorce. I'm not absolutely certain what caused it to break up. The other man grew into a different person. That may be the reason. George said he wants a long-term relationship. I hope he'll find someone who complements him. I don't know what type of person that would be. I think one day he'll find someone.

We spoke with one gay man, Jonathan, who had given considerable thought to the problems faced by parents in extending total acceptance to their gay and lesbian children. He brought up some concerns that are rarely talked about but are often thought about.

After getting over their hope that we can change, most parents worry that we'll lead lonely, unhappy lives. So they hope we'll find a nurturing partner. One of the most oppressive things, for a gay man at least, is the pressure from parents to adopt a full-formed, marriage-type relationship. The pressure is for a discreet, lifelong relationship—if possible, with some very "successful" partner.

Parents seem to resist any idea of a couple relationship that is not modeled after the ideal of heterosexual marriage. The fact is that gay male couples may be devoted and loving, but they are sometimes, often with permission from one another, non-monogamous. Some devoted gay male couples are able to do this without damaging their primary relationship, but this is upsetting to most parents. Whether we like it or not, heterosexual couples are sometimes non-monogamous too, but they are more secretive about it.

There are so many double standards. The widespread deviation from "the ideal" by heterosexuals is taken in stride, but very similar actions by gays are viewed as shameful. In California, where I live now, marriages last on the average something like five to seven years. So the real world of heterosexuals is more like a string of serial relationships— with or without marriage. I even heard a woman at a Santa Monica cocktail party say, "Oh, she'll make a lovely first wife for him."

If gays change partners at some similar rate, parents view it with special sorrow and dismay. The implication is that gays are "just promiscuous," and can't have serious, prolonged relationships. The fact is that many of them do, and they are highly caring and loving. Though again, if it is not 100 percent monogamous, it is considered peculiar or destructive. Parents need to remember that gays are denied any legal or spiritual equivalent of marriage. Imagine the straight world under those circumstances.

When families get together at Christmas or other holidays, talk goes on about a breakup or divorce of this couple or that. But the breakup of a gay couple is viewed as unseemly, and is given the old hush-hush treatment. So, as I say, if parents lay on us some unrealistic ideals which aren't lived up to even in the straight world—then to me it is oppression.

For example, a lot of gays are finding non-monogamous sex unsatisfying. If they felt they would not be met with hurt or lectures, they would welcome the chance to rethink freely this important part of their lives. They respect the life experiences of their parents, and they know their parents aren't saints. Maybe the hunger for honest talk could help all of them.

Jonathan also discussed the special questions that parents have about the lovers of their gay children. His conclusion at the end of the quote is a good one for answering the questions that parents bring up.

I know that the subject of lovers heightens tension for parents and brings up all kinds of questions. For example: As parents, how do you talk to the lover your gay child brings home? Do you acknowledge they are lovers? Do you raise the question about who will sleep where? If the lover has children, do you invite them to your home? Do you send them birthday cards? Do you ever talk about, or with, the parents of the lover? Will you meet them? What if there are religious differences? How do you introduce lovers to the relatives? Can you relate to the lover with honest feelings, or are you up-tight because of guilt about gayness? How do you react to conflicts in the relationship? Or breakups? Or the introduction of a new lover?

All in all, it's a tough ball game. It comes down to one thing though. If parents can see gays as just people, and gays can see parents as people, then we can work together on all these questions—like any adults who care about one another.

RESULTS OF SHARING

While many of our parents chose to share the fact of their child's homosexuality with the rest of the family, some others did not. We do not recommend that everyone necessarily can or should tell other members of the family. In thinking about all of the stories we heard, we came to the conclusion that parents did best when they listened to their own hearts. When the time and circumstances felt reasonably comfortable, the parents let the others know.

Those who did were pleased with the results. There often was created a feeling of family security that gave support to all its members. It was a support that was strong and unyielding to outside pressure. As the gay member received honest acceptance, each family member felt he or she was accepted too.

I feel closer to everyone I've told in the family. I also notice they are willing to tell me about their own concerns. The whole family seems more honest and aware of each other's needs. We're more like good friends. To the question "How are you?" I hear more real answers than "Just fine."

I should have had enough sense to realize that no family fits the "perfect" image. It's not necessary to get your self-esteem from that sort of thing.

Because my son turned out to be gay, I was forced to give up that hurtful idea of conforming to a fake image. I'm glad I was forced to do it because it helped me get more in touch with myself and with all my children. I think it even had a good effect on my marriage. To some extent we had been living an illusion, and now that is gone.

Having a gay person in the family has strengthened all of us. For a few months we tottered a bit. In fact, it was very rocky. We know now that we will give each other support for the rest of our lives. Oh, sometimes we are critical and irritable and have family blowups, but when the smoke dies down we come back together again.

chapter 8

Levels
of Understanding

*The way you feel and act now about your child's gayness is not the
way you will feel and act next year.*

Parents went through stages as they progressed in their
journey of understanding, acceptance, and beyond. We call
these stages "levels of understanding." At each level, parents
focused on different aspects of the issue—first on themselves,
then on their gay or lesbian child, and finally on gays and
lesbians everywhere.

In the beginning, parents have a need to get control of
their feelings while maintaining contact with their gay child.
We describe this focus as "Level I Understanding." When
parents are at this level, they direct their actions and attentions
primarily towards themselves. Easing their own inner conflict
is their prime goal.

As the work continues, there is a gradual change of
emphasis. After finding comfort and getting accurate infor-

mation, the parents begin to reach out to their gay child. They want to understand their child's needs, problems, and strengths. Their own needs take a back seat. When this occurs, parents have moved to "Level II Understanding."

Once parents take care of themselves and recognize where their child fits into the scheme of things, they are ready for another move. They begin to broaden their concern to include the welfare of all gay people. This signals that parents have reached "Level III Understanding."

These levels are a somewhat predictable educational pattern as parents learn not only to accept but also to appreciate their child's gayness. Getting all kinds of facts, changing their inner perceptions, and telling others enables parents to move through their levels of understanding. The whole process is like the educational system where children advance from primary to secondary and then to higher levels by learning history, math, and reading throughout their school years.

Not all the parents interviewed went through all levels because they entered the situation from a variety of backgrounds and circumstances. Overall, their movement through the levels was a long-term process. Some parents who previously had known gay or lesbian people moved faster. Also, involvement with a parents of lesbians and gays group early in the understanding process helped speed it along.

Another important factor for faster learning was the support that gay and lesbian children gave these parents during their time of confusion. The children answered questions about themselves and their private lives, reassured parents about cause, presented an assured manner, and understood their parents' feelings. Sometimes it was hard for the children to hear their parents express homophobic fears and concerns. But their patience was rewarded. Over and over parents also expressed appreciation for the understanding, education, and care their children provided.

All parents interviewed became aware of a reciprocal gain that developed as each level evolved. One mother summed it up when she said, "As we worked to understand and accept our children, we learned a lot about understanding and accepting ourselves." Let us examine more closely the three levels of understanding, as experienced and described by our parents.

LEVEL I: SELF-CENTERED CONCERN

At this level parents were concerned primarily with their own grief, and rightly so. They were reacting to an all-encompassing sense of loss. As with all major losses, parents at Level I had to mourn. Their self-centeredness at this period sometimes caused parents to feel ashamed and their gay or lesbian child to feel impatient. But mourning is a tough experience, and this self-concern is the necessary first step towards seeing the issue in a new light.

Parents were gripped by society's negative view, and homosexuality was thought to be abnormal. Yet, they often longed that somehow society could be different. There was little communication with anyone, even spouses. Marital relationships were strained. However, within a few days most mothers communicated with a close friend. Fathers usually did not even do that, perhaps because they had been taught to handle crises alone. Opposite sex parents of gay children sometimes had a sense of rejection. Same sex parents often felt they failed to provide the proper role modeling. Overall, parents pretty much isolated themselves, although the lucky ones found a parents' group and attended a meeting.

As for facts, parents started at ground zero. Most of their information was inaccurate. Many were too embarrassed even to get information from the local libraries or book stores.

In the beginning they rarely took a stand on gayness. Instead they felt at the mercy of the prevailing misinformation. Jokes and prejudicial comments caused severe anxiety. Fear, for themselves as well as for their gay or lesbian child, was a constant companion. There was a period of paranoia when parents felt they too would be ostracized. Religious attacks against homosexuality were terrifying to them.

Getting beyond Level I took the greatest effort, since they were emotionally weak, their information was inaccurate, and their isolation was great. But there was intense conflict between what society said about their gay child and what they instinctively knew about this same child. The pain of the conflict motivated parents to make new moves. They became open to helpful information and ignored biased opinions. They expressed a deep commitment towards continuing a mutually satisfying relationship with their child. With time and effort they graduated to the next level.

LEVEL II: CHILD-CENTERED CONCERN

Adjusting parents slowly found they were concentrating more and more of their concern on their child. They were surprised to find themselves operating at this level. Negative feelings were not as intense. Even though parents had "blue" days, the setbacks were temporary. When being completely honest, parents still wished their child were not gay, and they still had some trouble with the sexual aspects. But what was of more concern for them were the problems society imposed on that child.

Because parents were less self-centered, they were now willing to reach out and help other parents. Many attended meetings of gays and lesbians and shared their stories in the hope of helping other young people who were deciding to come out.

At this point, parents told us the relationship with their own child was getting better. Usually these children also reported a sense of relief at seeing their parents improve. Their worst fears of being rejected had not materialized, and they often felt they were back in the family circle. Parents became deeply aware of how difficult it had been for their gay or lesbian child and their main goal was to provide a haven for the child.

Parents now pursued the facts with zeal. They learned to read carefully and to examine the source of both positive and negative statements. They discovered that the negative view was usually prejudicial opinion, whereas a positive outlook was more likely to come from accurate information. Parents became convinced that society was far too harsh on the gay and lesbian community.

Most parents had come out to their close friends, but few had told grandparents and other extended family members. There were times when some would stand up publicly. They would speak for gay rights in the media if they could be anonymous. In general, the parental message was "I have a gay child and it is okay with me—just don't let them know my last name." The more exposure that parents had to standing up for their children, the more likely they were to move to the last level of understanding.

LEVEL III: CONCERN FOR ALL GAYS AND LESBIANS AND THEIR PARENTS

At this level, the parents had no doubt that an injustice had been perpetrated on gays and lesbians. The parents analyzed their own situation and abilities, and within that framework took some action.

Their struggle helped them feel stronger, both individually and as a group. In the absence of any role model these parents had to create new values and guideposts based on the reality of having gay children. It was a frightening place to be, but it was powerful and sometimes exhilarating.

Parents now saw real benefits from the situation. They no longer thought the lives of their gay and lesbian children should be carbon copies of their own, and they related to their gay children as they did to their nongay children. They found satisfaction from friendships with other gay and lesbian people. If they were in self-help groups, they had formed close friendships that they valued highly.

Now, sure of their facts, they were not threatened by different opinions. They regularly looked for opportunities to inform the misinformed. From this point on, parents committed themselves to standing against the prevailing negative view. Their stand was incorporated into the fabric of their lives. They did not allow jokes or disparaging remarks to go unchallenged. They were not afraid of criticism. A few even went on television with their story and their facts. Often they were more out than the children, since they would suffer no legal discrimination.

Two of the parents we interviewed illustrate clearly this movement through the levels. Helen gives a wide variety of details, while Jack describes fully how his inner perception changed.

HELEN'S STORY*

Helen is a white, middle class, schoolteacher who has been married for twenty-eight years to the same man. Both parents have devoted time and energy to their three children and enjoyed it. It is the oldest son who is gay.

Our son came out to us when he was seventeen years old. I remember that he said, "Mom and Dad, I'm gay. You've always thought you've known a lot about me, and you do. Now you know one thing more. It's important to me that you know all about my life and that you be able to share it with me." I had a numb feeling. It was a shock. I didn't want to have heard it. John and Craig began talking, and John was upset. Craig was calm. I didn't say much.

We went to my sister's as soon as we got dressed. She helped us because she accepts gayness as a natural way of life. While we were there John got down on his knees and begged Craig not to act on his homosexuality. I remember John saying, "If you really are a homosexual it will be okay, but you don't know for sure. You're too young." But, in fact, everyone knew there was no question about Craig's being gay.

During this time I was not involved. I just watched everything that was going on. John and my sister and Craig were interacting, but I was not. Later on that day I saw a boy and girl walking in the park holding hands. I knew Craig would never do that. My eyes teared up, and a heavy feeling settled on my chest. That feeling stayed with me for a long time.

---

*This is the mother's version of finding out that was told by the father at the opening of Chapter 1.

Helen made an early and crucial decision to accept her son's homosexuality as an undeniable fact. Then she began to change herself by examining her feelings and belief system in detail. This is an important decision that allows parents not to waste time on futile dreams.

I was very self-centered. I did not deal with my son. I don't like saying that. I would like to think that I was kind and understanding as I reached out towards Craig, but I wasn't. I was hurting, and I didn't understand why it hurt so much. I didn't think about Craig for a good while. In fact it was some time before I realized what a traumatic experience he had gone through.

I was ashamed and that was a first for me concerning my children. There was little help. I told my sister and one friend, and that was it. I thought we were the only couple on the face of the earth that ever had a gay child.

I used to sit and listen to gay jokes and cringe, but I said nothing. More than once I had to leave a room to keep from crying. I gained a lot of weight and felt very depressed. I was lonely.

Parents often fear for themselves as well as for their children. They see themselves facing the same kind of rejection their gay children have had to face.

Because I'm a teacher, I was afraid that if the people in the town found out about my son I would have a lot of problems with my job. I even thought I might get fired. At the time I definitely felt I had caused Craig's homosexuality. So it made sense to me that it was not the homosexual who should be fired, but the parent.

Helen found herself monitoring the most common actions. This was an unsettling experience.

One of the biggest problems we had with our son's homosexuality had to do with rules. All the little social rules that we knew so well didn't seem to fit. There were no guideposts. We didn't know how to react to him and his lover. We questioned how we would all act around his grandparents. We were in trouble, but we didn't know where to turn.

For a while we had no idea even how to talk about Craig. General conversations with our family and friends became a chore.

Parental concern for their own sexuality is very common, and for some it creates a sense of insecurity. It may be the prime reason for extremely negative reactions.

After I found out that Craig was gay, I thought about sexuality a lot. And I worried about mine. I never really had any doubts about my heterosexuality, but there was a little part of me that was afraid. When I was in school, there was a term called "latent homosexuality." My understanding of this term was that a person could be sitting on an unknown time bomb that could go off if just the right set of circumstances came about. And there wouldn't be any inkling that you were gay unless those circumstances happened. I remember thinking, "I have good women friends. Does that mean I could be gay?" Now I realize what a silly and homophobic thought that was.

The search for cause motivated by her guilt occupied much of Helen's thoughts for some time.

When Craig came out to us, I thought that homosexuality was a mental problem of some kind. So his being gay was a crushing blow—a gut level failure. I thought, "What am I here for if I did this to my baby?" I didn't know how, I didn't know when, I didn't know what I had done. I searched through his growing-up years, but nothing seemed to fit what I'd read.

Still, the finger of guilt pointed straight at me. I have trouble finding the words to say how bad I felt. But I wanted someone to take away my pain. I wanted someone to ease my burden of guilt.

After a while, I began to cope a little. I found out some information and began to see things more realistically. Although I began to feel better, the low times still came. For a long time I had more bad days than good. I'd have to catch hold of myself and fight the old fears repeatedly.

I have always been in a series of roles. I've been a daughter, wife, mother, teacher. Without one of these roles to give me support I didn't know how to act. It was important for me to be successful in all of them.

When I found out my son was gay, a funny thing happened. Not only was my mothering role tested and found wanting, but so was my role as a wife.

On top of thinking I had failed my son, I felt like I had failed John because his son was not the all-American boy. I needed John to reassure me about this and to convince me I wasn't a failure to him and the rest of the family.

He couldn't do that. At that time he wanted me to assure him that he wasn't a failure as a father. Neither of us could make the pain go away for the other.

Ideally we should have been leaning on one another and giving support. In truth we didn't give each other any help at all. I wanted to be a little girl and be petted, and understood and allowed to cry. But he couldn't let me do that because he was suffering the same way I was.

For some time I was withdrawn from John and he was from me. It was as if we each went off into a shell somewhere. Neither of us could understand why we were so hurt. We couldn't understand why we were so fearful, and we felt bad about feeling that way.

Just before Craig told us, I can remember thinking, "We're like one of those ideal TV families. We have one girl and two boys. They're all on the honor roll at school. John and I have a good relationship. Life just can't be better. We did it. We've done a good job." For a while it looked like our world was full of roses. But after we found out that Craig was gay, all the roses wilted.

Everyone in the family had a hard time. We went from having a perfect family image to being just a bunch of individuals who peeped out at each other and said, "Why don't you make it better for me?" None of us was able to do that. We all wanted to, but everyone was too weak. We were not a good support system at that time.

This mother next reported actions which started her movement from a self-centered stage to an understanding of her son's position.

For a good while I wondered if my grief would ever be completely over. I suffered the death of a dream. A part of it was being a good mother according to what my neighbors would think. I wanted to be accepted and looked up to by society. But there was more to this grief than that. I've had trouble figuring out what it was all about.

I got some help. I talked to a counselor. It was good just to talk it through. But you have to be careful whom you talk to. You want someone who understands homosexuality and accepts it as a positive way of life.

Craig helped us right after he told us; also later on as we began to understand what had happened. He was able to reassure us on almost everything that we were afraid of.

He constantly forced us to face up to the fact that he was gay. He insisted on being the person he was. He started pressing early to bring his boyfriend home. We didn't want him to, but Craig brought him home anyway. We liked him and we liked the way they acted towards each other. Seeing their mutual care and concern eased our fear that Craig would always be lonely.

Now as I think back over it, I am filled with a feeling of being loved by Craig. It must have been hard for him to see his parents react as negatively as we did. But his self-confidence made us both feel better. It still does.

When I think of how it was for him, I feel sad. Craig first discovered he was gay when he was thirteen. He said that at night he would lie in bed and cry because he knew what he was, and he could not change it. He got lonelier and lonelier. He tried to do everything really well, and he received honors throughout high school. But his loneliness would not go away. He's a very attractive kid, and a lot of girls were after him. He saw girls during that whole time, trying to cover up, trying to get interested in a female. But he couldn't. I wish John and I could have helped him more.

Having worked through some of her early grieving, this mother made another decision that is typical of parents in the middle level of understanding. She decided to take a risk and tell someone else about her situation. This led to the major source of help for her—other parents.

I was taking a class on sexism in education at a local college. Following one of our class discussions, the teacher asked if we would like to learn something about homosexuality. Most people in the room agreed that they would.

After class, when the professor was alone in front of the room, I got up enough courage to tell her about Craig. There were tears in my eyes as I talked. She didn't say anything, just reached over and took my hand. I still remember the feel of her hand on mine. She looked gently at me. She understood. I didn't have to tell her anything else. It was a beautiful moment.

Soon after, a gay man came to talk to our class. He was sure of himself and seemed very well put together as a person. Most of all he was proud of himself. Meeting him made me feel better. I guess that was the first time I began to see homosexuality as just another way of living. He made it okay for me.

Later he took John and me over to a parents' group meeting. I sat and cried. The people there understood. John talked too, and we were not alone. We became just two of many who were fighting for our children.

In general, each time a parent chooses to tell someone about having a gay son or lesbian daughter, the chains of prejudice are loosened.

Telling is a big decision for parents. It certainly was for me. John and I had a big disagreement over telling his folks. We never did, and I don't feel as close to them. I felt forced to choose between them and my child, and I resented it.

Every time I told someone about Craig's being gay, I felt stronger. I'm not sure why. Maybe it was because I was in control, and I was supporting Craig.

Helen's son has moved back into his accustomed role in family situations and Helen has now reached Level III. She accepts her gay son, her parenting, and other gays and lesbians.

Now Craig can tell us pretty much anything he wants to. He expects us to love him, no matter what. And that's an expectation we've met. He's our son, and we love him just like he is.

I worry about him the way I worry about my other two children. I think he is very courageous and strong as a gay person in this society. He doesn't let prejudicial statements get him down. If he does have problems he feels he can handle them. I think he can. He doesn't make the situation worse than it is.

You know, a funny thing happened about this idea of love. All of our children say that we love them more than parents usually love their children. I think it's because we were tested, and we passed. Our children have no doubts that we will accept them for what they are.

When I look back over my progress since I found out that Craig was gay, I realize that I expected myself to be too accepting too soon. I didn't give myself the right to have bad feelings. I condemned them instead. My basic feelings for Craig are caring, love and concern. I have felt those since he was born. They will not change. I would have been better off had I just given myself the right to explore my negative feelings.

Now I think that John and I are good parents. We provided a good climate for our children to grow up in.

A few months ago our parent group met with a group of gay teenage boys. As I sat and listened to their sad stories of loneliness and rejection, I felt ashamed. I thought, "I was a part of hurting these youngsters when I believed it was wrong to be gay. I kept quiet when I heard derogatory remarks. These boys don't deserve this." That evening I moved all the way over. All my prejudice went away. Now I think of those children as being my children, and I'm going to do everything I can to help make this a better place for them.

Lately I've even told some parents of the students I teach in school. I will appear on TV or on radio if I'm asked. I'm not too worried about what other people think, and I feel stronger and more sure of myself. I am proud of the way John and I have handled the whole situation.

I've had to face a mountain of prejudice against homosexuality. Some of it was inside me and some of it was out there in the town where I live. The climb has given me a hardy sense of worthiness. I've begun to look at all my thinking more carefully. I feel more in charge of my life.

The mountain hasn't been totally climbed. I suspect it never will be. When I think I'm at the top, another hill appears and I have to go over that. But I'm not afraid of those hills. They're small in comparison to the enormous mountain that I've already conquered.

JACK'S STORY*

Jack is a sixty-three-year-old professor at a prestigious university in the Midwest He has known about his son's gayness

---

*This is the father's version of finding out described earlier by the mother in Chapter 1.

for nine years. He and his wife, who have three children, helped form a parents' group in their town. Chris, their middle child and only son, is gay.

When Chris decided to tell his parents about his gayness, he tried to find ways to ease the sense of loss that he expected them to feel. He had thoughtfully provided counseling help for the family and this got them started on the right foot. Though Jack's initial reaction was mild, he quickly saw the need to face his negative feelings honestly and openly. This action is a lot easier to say than do. Few of us want to admit that we have trouble accepting something basic about our children.

In the next few quotes Jack clearly describes the beginning level of understanding. He was primarily concerned with himself and his feelings.

I remember when Chris told us he was gay. We were stunned, and for a time his announcement was followed by silence. Then he started to cry. I just went over and put my arms around him.

I was shaken by it. I had a lot of mixed feelings. Chris was in training as a clinical psychologist, and he had talked with a therapist about the possibility of our coming to see him. The whole family went the next day. That was a big help. We got feelings out. Part of me was kind of numb. I hadn't really accepted it, but having a chance to talk it out was a lucky break. It was a useful thing for that immediate occasion, but it didn't get me around the corner in terms of really accepting homosexuality.

Fairly soon we flew back home, and got in touch with the local gay church to find out if there was a parents' group. There wasn't, but we were invited to attend one of their services.

The church service really shook me. I had trouble fighting back the tears during the service. There were gay and lesbian couples going up to the altar together holding hands. I wasn't feeling positive about that. I was thinking, "Is Chris going to be into something like this?" I was feeling sorry for myself that that would happen. But I had all sorts of mixed feelings, because I also thought there were very tender feelings between these people.

Then when they were singing hymns like the ones in the Methodist Church I grew up in, I began having flashbacks. I wondered how my mother would have experienced this. It was a Christian service, but with something "peculiar" going on. I don't think she could have handled it. I was having strong feelings during the service, fighting back tears the whole time.

As is typical with many fathers of gay sons, Jack remembers trying to develop a father/son relationship with the usual male pursuits.

I had had bad feelings about our relationship when Chris was growing up. I felt a failure. I couldn't seem to make contact with him. He seemed irritated with me a lot and I'd get irritated with him.

I kept trying to get Chris into playing catch, and he just wasn't interested. So I thought, "Okay, don't lay my trip on him. Let him be where he is."

Later I then tried to get him interested in Boy Scouts. He had no interest in that either. I don't think we went to more than three or four meetings.

The scouts had a father and son overnight that fall. We were in pup tents, and there was an early snow. Chris got sick and had to be taken home during the night. It just seemed like nothing was working.

In the next quote we are given a good example of a parent who is moving into the middle level of understanding (the child-centered stage). He is very aware of the needs of his son and of his own needs.

For a while after finding out, Marilyn and I had a tendency not to talk about it. It was easier to talk about anything else. Finally, we agreed that the subject would be one we would actively bring up. We began to move.

When Chris came home the first time after telling us, he probed about where we were in our understanding. He wanted us to assure him that we totally accepted his homosexuality. We both said we couldn't— that we hadn't made our peace with it yet. We didn't give him anything phony. He had to accept us where we were.

That was one of the first corners we got around. It was a critical step for all of us to stay with reality. Being exactly where we were was the most caring thing we could do. He had been honest with us when he came out and that set the tone for how we had to deal with each other.

At some point I decided that I had to make- some kind of adjustment about his gayness. I could not become fixated on my own misery and discomfort. I had to let go of it. I didn't like it, but gradually I decided it was his life.

I've moved to the point where I can deal honestly with Chris. We can be open about one of the heaviest of issues, homosexuality. It's a number one challenge, because I started as far back as anyone.

All the ideas I had of homosexuality were negative. It was something I don't remember ever talking about. My image was that gays were people who picked up sex in the park. It was dirty and was done by people with strange mannerisms. Then I realized that I, myself, was now associated with gayness. My child was into something that repels a lot of people. I'm now part of it.

So, my feelings about homosexuality in general were riding heavily on my shoulders. They were wrapped around me and I had trouble getting them off.

Rather than continuing to put himself down for not being perfect in this whole process, Jack accepts himself where he is.

Perfectionism is a tyranny that I've had trouble shaking. I thought I had to give up all my negative feelings in order to have a good relationship with Chris. But anger and negative feelings are just a part of living. There's always ambivalence. Right now, I say I'll probably always have wishes that he weren't a homosexual. He's without a partner and I often think he will have a lonely kind of battle.

While I still have my hang-ups about homosexuality, I know we also have moved closer to each other. I feel good that Chris and I can hug each other. He now says he wants us to live near him in California. When I think about how much of a failure I felt in relation to Chris when he was growing up, I find these changes remarkable.

If Jack had stopped here, he and Chris would probably be reasonably comfortable together. But he made a deliberate choice to continue working. A year later Jack reported further movement in his relations with Chris.

Significant changes have continued to take place. Until about a year ago I harbored many regrets. I still thought if I had a choice, I would want Chris to be heterosexual. Even after all my involvement in the parents' group, I joined the long line of parents who said, "Of course we wouldn't choose it for our child."

I've gotten away from that, and I'm trying to get in touch with why. I think it has to do with what has happened and with a change of perception about what really has been good for my life and for Chris. But the changes came only after some hard discussions with him.

One summer evening around the fire at our mountain cabin in Colorado, I told Chris of my continuing distaste for the sexual acts between men.

He was hurt that I would come back with statements and feelings out of the old places. It was hard for him to hear me go back to these harsh messages. But he knew they were in me, and he was willing to face the issues once again.

In these tough confrontations with Chris I got into the real nitty-gritty. I can't recount all the details, but as we talked I heard myself realizing truths about sex that I had pushed aside. Chris pointed out that nongays engage in the same sexual behaviors which are condemned for gays, and that therefore the image of "dirty" that I had associated with gay sex was also valid for heterosexual sex.

I became aware that I had resisted acknowledging these facts. I have mixed feelings about the whole sexual revolution. Deeply rooted within me is the traditional western teaching that only heterosexual sex is okay. But I also know that I welcome for myself a wider range of sexual expression, including what I was condemning in gay people. I began to realize how hypocritical I was being. I finally could laugh at myself.

Jack then expressed feelings that come to parents who have moved beyond acceptance. It is a level that has its own reward.

I have come to realize that my son's being gay has been a major source of personal liberation for me. I grew up in a conservative, German neighborhood with the message: "Keep in mind what the neighbors will think." I have gradually come to realize how crippling and burdensome that message is. It asked me not to look at the world through my own eyes and not to face the truth about my life as I experienced it. I spent too much of my energy trying to keep up appearances.

If Chris had not been gay, I would have let life cheat me. In a very real sense he rescued me from that. I am freer now to take other risks as I face what I want to do with my life.

It is Chris' nature to be gay. That is the way he came into the world, and the way he is in the world. I would never change him even if I could. He and all the other gay and lesbian children have a right to be here as they are. They can help us expand our lives by widening the range of differences that we can embrace and enjoy.

Learning to appreciate being parents of lesbian and gay children is a process, not an end point. Our society continually changes and adjusted parents have the capacity and self-confidence to grow and change as the need arises.

chapter *9*

Contrast and Comparison of What Was and What Will Be

I have a fantasy about America in twenty more years. I'll be eighty then. I'll be this little old lady who, back in the 1980s worked for gay people's rights. Instead of saying, "You were brave," I hope they'll say, "Gay rights? You mean they haven't always had rights? Are you sure you're not making this up?" I look forward to the time when the parents' organization will be out of business, no longer needed.

When I look at him, I sometimes want to cry because I'm so proud of the way he handled it when everyone in the world told him he wasn't okay. I can hardly believe one of my children had that much courage, awareness, ability, self-confidence, to know he was okay. Even when we were doubtful, he didn't lash back at us. He just went on.

It has been a hard struggle. But finally we have come to see gayness as a gift instead of a curse.

155

IMAGES OF THE FUTURE

The following quotations present a direct picture of the future that parents want to come about. They are good examples of what "beyond acceptance" really means.

Some day homosexuality will be taken as much for granted as heterosexuality. People will not only accept gay rights as ordinary, they'll say, "Why did it take us so long to come to our senses?"

When we parents speak publicly, the audiences are frozen with interest. There is no sound, no movement. I hope someday that will change, that people will be bored with it all and say, "What was all the fuss about? Of course some people are gay. What of it?"

It is my hope that in challenging the lies, myths, and gossip about gay people, we'll create a new generation of parents. These parents will have such accurate information about homosexuality that they won't see it as an unusual or threatening thing if one or more of their children turns out to be gay. It will be more like having a curly-haired child or a straight-haired one, a tall one or a short one.

To me homosexuality is not a matter of right and wrong. It's just a part of the way things are. We all have our daily way of life. We're not used to all the new things we've been learning the past few years. But because of TV, radio, and other media, we hear more about different ways of life than we ever have in the past.

I think that within fifteen or twenty years this whole issue about homosexuality will be a dead issue. Our society has gone through this with all different ethnic groups as they came into the country. When I was a child, Jewish people were considered strange exotic people in my neighborhood. Blacks were the same. Catholics were suspect. Even left-handed people were looked down on. Every kind of person who is different, unfortunately, has had to go through this. Now the gay people are going through it. But I have no doubt that they will come out on the other side if we keep working and educating and raising people's awareness.

The next generation of parents should have much better informa-tion and preparation for dealing with a gay child. I don't want other families to have to suffer and struggle to get information like we did.

CHANGES IN PARENTAL ATTITUDES

When parents are helped to escape from their closet, perhaps one toe at a time, they enter a world of new pos-sibilities—a new perception of the world. It is one which is exciting and satisfying. The following statements show this before and after change:

What parents said at first: Don't tell a soul. Cover it up. Lie if necessary. What they said later: How can I ask anyone to deny the basic sexual orientation of his or her life? How would I like to be made to feel ashamed of my heterosexuality? If other people condemn, it's because they know nothing about the facts.

At first: *Why should we change? We're not the ones with the problem.*
Later: *I realize now I did have a problem. I thought my way was the only way to be. I found that prejudice, though hard to give up, was an enormous burden.*

At first: *Don't make us question our religion.*
Later: *My religion means even more to me now, and presents no conflict. I realized the real message of all religions is to love, not judge, those who are different from me.*

At first: *Above all, don't show your affection for your lover in front of us or the relatives.*
Later: *You have a right to express affection the same as our straight children, no more, no less. The family customs of "good taste" should operate on a single standard.*

At first: *If you must be gay, then try to be perfect in every other way, to compensate.*

Later: *You can be yourself, imperfect like the rest of us. Strong in some areas, not so strong in others. We love you as you are. If we have gripes, we'll talk them out the same as we would with any other loved one.*

At first: *How could you do this to me? Do you realize the pain this is causing?*

Later: *My pain forced me to face the conflict between myths I'd been taught, and scientific facts about homosexuality. Some of the pain stems from my own resistance to change. Accepting differences in others helps me to be kinder to myself, to accept my own differences.*

At first: *I can't bear to risk the rejection of my relatives, friends or neighbors, by admitting I have a gay child.*

Later: *I found that the relatives, friends, and neighbors that I care about like me more when I can follow my own conscience, and not be dependent on their opinions.*

CHANGES IN PARENTS' PERCEPTIONS OF GAYNESS

The fundamental changes that took place in the lives of accepting parents were reflected in their everyday language. We now listen to them describe, with personal detail, their new way of perceiving the world of their gay children.

Society says our gay children are disturbed, weak, and immoral. I find them to be mature, of high principles, and persistently of strong character. Others say gay people are ridiculous or outrageous. I find them to be loving, sensitive, both serious and humorous. "They" call them failures. I find successes. Gays and lesbians are called unmanly or unwomanly. I find them deep, fully developed men and women.

I don't want her to be alone. I'm glad she found someone. It's her life. If she's happy, that's the important thing.

Everyone doesn't live like you do, or like I do. Everyone has a different way. There are so many different life styles. Being gay is just one more of them. I don't approve of it for me, but that doesn't mean it's wrong.

One friend asked me, "Wouldn't you like it better if he wasn't gay?" And I can very honestly say "no." It doesn't matter a bit. Paul is Paul. Once I got past the stage of thinking of all the terrible things that crazy people with guns might do to him...when I got past that, I no longer cared that he was gay. If he were somebody else...if he were straight, maybe he'd be different. And I don't want him different in any way. This is him. Being gay is part of him. He's a wonderful young man. Now I confess, I do wish he'd stand up straight. He's going to have a bad back by the time he's thirty.

I feel very good toward Ken. It never crosses my mind that he might change some day, or wouldn't it be nice if he were to change. I really don't care about that. That's a dead issue. We get along very well. Of course, he lives a distance away which makes it easier to get along, because we're not involved in any nitty-gritty daily problems. But still, when we're together, we're immediately in tune with one another. It's a good feeling. And I see his life style as perfectly okay. I still think it's inconvenient in our society, but that's not his fault. I don't think he's done anything wrong. I regret, to put it mildly, that our society penalizes gays and their families.

WHY GAY PEOPLE WANT TO COME OUT TO PARENTS

As gay people gain self-pride, they get tired and impatient with having to maintain old deceptions. They don't want to be treated better than their heterosexual brothers and sisters. They simply want to be accepted as they were accepted when they were children—as human beings who have the same right to be here with their special uniqueness as any other person on earth. That's another reason for their deep need to tell parents—"to find out if I'm loved for who I really am." The following quotations, one from a gay man, and one from a lesbian, poignantly convey their need to come out to their families:

In growing up, I had experienced life about like other kids. Some problems, of course, but in general I was just another part of the family, of school life, and of the rest of the world. When I gradually discovered I wasn't like my peers, that I might be gay, all of this that I had been able to take for granted began to change.

In many ways, I felt less than a whole person, even though I hadn't shared my feelings with a single soul. I was now one of those "terrible people." I took in the feeling that there was something dreadfully wrong with me—something so awful that if it was discovered, I might lose the parental love I was so dependent on for a good part of my existence. Or, because of this deeply awful thing about myself, I might be a source of great hurt to my parents. I longed to tell them and to be told I was loved, no matter what.

After my sister had put her children to bed, I sat down with her and after a few minutes finally blurted out, "Sherry, what I wanted to tell you is that I'm gay." She replied, "Well, okay" and took the news in a calm manner.

Then she said she had a question to ask me, and said, "I don't think it's any of my affair what your sexual life is like. I don't talk about my sexual life to anybody, and I don't see why you need to even worry about whether to tell us or not. What is all this business about gay people wanting to come out of the closet? Why tell people what you're doing? Why on earth would you people want to talk about it?"

I explained that it's because of the prejudice against us. We feel that we cannot be openly seen to be affectionate with a member of the same sex. We fear loss of our jobs or status or friendships. Whereas if you're married, you're openly with your beloved all the time. And that's the way it's "supposed to be." When you're heterosexual, you don't have to talk about your sex life because your sexuality is understood and affirmed automatically.

I also spoke about my sense of alienation from the family gatherings when everyone was together with their spouses and their families. The family gatherings were the worst times for me, because I had someone that I loved too, but I felt I couldn't say "Let me bring my partner. She's the one I really care about." So I felt I was the loner in the family.

WHY PARENTS NEED THEIR CHILDREN TO COME OUT TO THEM

When children are honest with their parents about being lesbian or gay, they risk a great deal. So those who tell their parents show strength of character and real love for them. They want the relationship to be marked by complete integrity. To have that, they must be out of the closet and up front about the reality of their lives. Without this kind of sharing, the individuals are like actors performing prescribed roles. They are not present to each other as the real persons they are.

Children come to their parents with trust as well as fear. They are telling themselves, "Even if my parents may not approve, they will be there for me. They will still love me, they will respect my sincerity, and they will take my comments seriously." That trust is a great compliment to a parent. It implies that a truly loving parent-child relationship exists. There is communication, love, caring, honesty, and a desire to let everyone in the relationship be who they are.

With trust present, even if approval is delayed, gay and lesbian people tend to be able to cope with any problem. So do the other family members. This doesn't mean they breeze through life easily. They have just as many serious problems as anyone else. But when confronted with a difficult situation, the family members search, bend, persist with all their strength until there is some resolution that is satisfactory to all.

As parents look back they realize they've made a connection in the deepest sense with their child. Listen as parents share this awareness.

It takes a lot of courage for our children to tell us. Particularly if they're close to us. That might seem to be a contradiction. But I think it's hard even for those who've had easy, good relationships with their parents, because they don't want to jeopardize that. And they don't want to hurt us. They think and hope we'll accept it. But they're not positive. I think it's important to realize that it's very special, their coming out to us. It's interesting that all the parents I know are not sorry their children told them, though they may have been at first. Even though some of them went through hell, they still prefer to know.

I know it was difficult for Mary to tell us; perhaps the most difficult thing she's ever had to do. She told us because she cares so much for us. She felt she had to tell us and I think she wanted to tell us. She wanted us to share in her happiness. I couldn't do that, when she first told us, but I can now.

Now that she's out in the open, she seems to feel good about herself. Her health is much better, and she's much more open in all her dealings and relationships, both inside and outside the family.

Young people who share their homosexuality with their families are not likely to enter into a marriage hoping it will make them heterosexual. They won't make themselves and someone else unhappy. I had a woman friend who was married six years to a man who was gay. She was utterly miserable. I'm sure he was too. She held some hope all those years, and even after she divorced him, that he could change. This kind of thing should not happen. And it probably won't happen if gay people have the love and support of their parents.

Everything that's important in your life that you share with someone you care about, intensifies your relationship. So it's made us closer even though we were close before. But if my daughter hadn't told me, and felt that she had to go her way on this, and I go mine, it would have been a barrier. Instead, knowing and sharing this has enriched our relationship. It also opens up a channel for other talk in the future. If we can share this kind of thing, then there is very little else she can't tell me. Or that I couldn't tell her.

Parents also want and need something from their gay children, something that may seem paradoxical at first. The parents we interviewed often said: "We wanted her/ him to give us time to adjust, to integrate the new information and to get used to a radical shift of thinking. But we also needed to be confronted firmly and gently if we ran away from the truth or if we were stalling, or were misinformed. So we told our gay child: 'Be firm in your belief in yourself, and in the honorableness of homosexuality. Tell us you love us, and that you want an open, honest relationship that continues indefinitely.'"

This can be summed up by one father's comment:

She had her life together and was happy. She was proud of being a gay person. Because she accepted herself, it helped give us courage to accept her and ourselves as being just fine the way we are.

GAY PEOPLE, PARENTS, AND SOCIETY

Our gay and lesbian children made clear beyond a doubt that parental support enriched their lives and helped them face a hostile world. Their self-acceptance was achieved more quickly and easily with parents' approval.

When parents supported their children, they supported and healed themselves, and built up their own self-esteem and self-confidence. Just as many gay people have insisted on an honest relationship with their parents, we hope that parents will insist on the same kind of honesty with the rest of society.

When society takes the step of dropping its hostility to such a large section of its own members, it will have made a major step towards furthering its own health—because it will have lowered the level of violent and destructive tendencies within itself.

Parents of my generation (age fifty and up) are apt to feel rejected when their child settles on a sexual orientation that is different from their own. I guess a lot of us have problems with accepting and valuing differences. This is not just a parents' problem, it's a cultural problem. That's why we have racism, and anti-Semitism, and strife between peoples. We haven't learned to appreciate deep fundamental dif-

ferences in a cooperative and friendly way. We see differences as threats to who we are.

The following is a statement from a young gay man who explains how the peace and caring restored within an accepting family can become a miniature representation for society.

We want to be out of the closet so that we can be close to our families. We don't want to waste energy covering up the basic facts of our lives. Also, we want to be out because some of our greatest strengths and talents can only be expressed freely when we are completely ourselves. When we are not out, to our families, to co-workers, to the world, the constraint that goes into hiding and the inner conflict that daily drains our energy spells a real waste of human intelligence, creativity, and sensitivity.

We want to make a better world for all people, but particularly for gay people in future generations. Most gay people I have talked with feel that their coming out is part of the historical moment. We feel this sense of responsibility and urgency to open things up so that those who come after us won't have to suffer as much as we did. Just like those before us in the forties and fifties, the Daughters of Bilitis, for example, or the men of the Mattachine Society, made possible this discussion that we're having now.

There's something about gay liberation and being open about homosexuality that reverberates far beyond the obvious questions of accepting a difference in sexual orientation. When gay people are out of the closet, the world's eyes are opened to a way of expressing human feeling that does not obey the old system in which only heterosexuality is acceptable. Our present system is one that restricts both men and women, whether heterosexual or homosexual. A calm, complete, and honest sex education dealing with all human diversity can help all children, all people. I'm not talking about the ways our society deals with sexuality through suggestive movies or advertising. This I see as pseudo-openness. All sexuality needs to be brought out in the open in a healthy way. A discussion of the true facts about homosexuality can bring heterosexuality into clearer focus. When we come out to our families we are raising these issues whether or not they are named.

We hope that in the future people will be less frightened and enraged by differences. Violence against gay people is due to fears about persons who are different, and to myths about dangers they represent. We simply want to be complete human beings without being objects of rage. We don't want special treatment, we want equal treatment. We are asking heterosexual people to accept the reality of homosexuality—to accept us simply as human beings, with the usual range of strengths and weaknesses.

An Interview: Mother and Gay Son

The following is a dialogue between a mother and a gay son, age twenty-four. It concerns what he hopes for in their parent-child relationship in the future. He also discusses the coming out process from his perspective seven years later. He tells what he liked and didn't like about the time he came out at age seventeen. The interview concentrates on the son's thoughts, feelings, and opinions. But there is a hidden message in the dialogue—that the mother could hear her son's past pain without being defensive. She showed empathy for his situation, and he showed empathy for hers.

Parent: *As a gay man, what do you expect of parents? Tell me first what you expect your dad and me to do. And then what you hope all parents would do for their children.*

Son: *I hope that you and Dad will just be supportive. And love me. I don't think that's a small thing. Just be my mom and dad—the same as you always have been. I guess that's what I want. I don't necessarily expect you to accept everything or to like everything about the gay life style. But I hope you'll try to understand another person's point of view and accept me as much as you do my brother and sister. That way you'll treat me as an individual.*

Parent: *When you came out to us, what did you expect?*

Son: *I expected you to get upset and then think it was okay.*

Parent: *Is that what happened?*

Son: *The time factor was a little different than what I expected.*

Parent: *It was a lot slower?*

Son: *Yes.*

Parent: *Is there anything you did during the time that your dad and I were having trouble with the process, that you thought was helpful to us?*

Son: *I guess I was firm. I think that was good. I didn't give in. But at the same time, I don't think I was obnoxious. And I tried to be helpful and provide you with information. I tried to convince you that I was actually the same person and that you just knew me a little better now.*

Parent: *When did you realize you were gay, whether you had a word for it or not?*

Son: *I was fairly positive by the time I was in sixth grade, because I had sexual thoughts about men instead of women. The other boys were talking about girls, and I was thinking about boys. When I was growing up I was different. And I was ridiculed constantly because I was different.*

Parent: *When do you remember feeling that you were different?*

Son: *I'm not sure—six years old, maybe five years old.*

Parent: *And what were you ridiculed about?*

Son: *Not being good in sports, and for being too feminine.*

Parent: *Called "sissy" and such as that?*

Son: *Yes, but you know, I'm sure every child feels special in a lot of ways. You talk to any gay guy, and he will tell you that he always felt different, even if he didn't know he was gay until he was much older. But I wonder if all children might feel different in some way. Almost everyone has trouble with their sexuality in one way or another. Many children might worry a lot and feel there's something wrong with them, including a large number who aren't gay. And certainly a lot of people who are called sissies don't grow up to be gay. But I think perhaps the insecurity is more intense for gay people.*

Parent: *You were seventeen when you came out to us and twelve when you knew for sure. Between the ages of twelve and seventeen, how was it for you?*

Son: *I thought my life was going to be miserable. And I thought I was sick. I was completely horrified by the immensity of my problem, and how isolated I felt. And there was no one I could talk to.*

Parent: *No one at all? Not one person?*

Son: *No one at all. I didn't talk to anyone until after I came out to myself, and I'd started having sex when I was seventeen.*

Parent: *That's about the same time you told us.*

Son: *Yes.*

Parent: *What during those years was helpful to you?*

Son: *I read a lot. I suppose that was the only thing. I didn't read anything that was helpful about being gay. All I did was bury myself in books because it was a way to escape from life. There was nothing at all that was helpful about being gay. Not a single, solitary thing.*

Parent: *What do you think inside you gave you the courage to come out when you did? You were pretty young.*

Son: *Well, I figured I had a choice. I could go on being miserable and dead inside or I could at least see if there was any possibility for me to have some kind of interest, some excitement or something sexual that I enjoyed out of my life. Perhaps emotional honesty was what I was after. I kept trying to tell myself it was a stage, and so on—the things gay people always tell themselves to avoid the truth. It took a long time for me to really accept it.*

Parent: *What advice would you give to young gay people that might help their lives as they're growing up?*

Son: *Well, stay off the streets. Try to find some kids your own age who are decent and who are gay, if you can. Form some kind of friendship with them. Try not to grow up in a little town.*

Parent: *I've been thinking about Alan, your first lover. He was very helpful to us. I wonder if we hurt him or your other friends in any way.*

Son: *I think you made them feel good.*

Parent: *How?*

Son: *By talking to them and being interested.*

Parent: *Now on the converse side, was there anything that we did that was hurtful when you came out? I don't want you to whitewash it.*

Son: *The thing that comes to mind, and I don't really blame you for it, was that you and Dad were so hung up about my being different from the time I was four years old. It was obvious that you both were disappointed by the whole notion that I might be gay, or at least different from the all-American kind of little boy. While I was still struggling with accepting myself, those memories magnified the inten-*

sity of the doubts and questions I had in my own head. I think this made it a lot worse for me. But I see you and Dad as having changed a lot.

Parent: *Do you have any idea as to what we did to change?*

Son: *I think you both reexamined the whole notion of sex roles. Those kinds of things.*

Parent: *How do you view your future as a gay man in this society? Do you think you're going to be hurt by it?*

Son: *Probably. But I just think of life as something to be gotten on with. You just try to do the best you can and muddle through. You hope for the best and see how things go.*

Parent: *From the gay people that you know, is it better to stay in the closet or come out of the closet?*

Son: *Come out of the closet. At least then you have the potential of being happy, more satisfied, and feeling that you're fulfilling your destiny and doing what you want to do. You're in charge of your life.*

Parent: *In other words, when you come out, you don't buy other people's negative view of homosexuality?*

Son: *I didn't say that. A lot of gay people do buy it. They take it out on themselves in a lot of different ways. But I think you at least have a lot more potential for enjoying your life and doing what you want to do if you're out of the closet. I wouldn't ever try to tell other gays to be open like me. That's an individual decision.*

Parent: *But you needed to come out of the closet?*

Son: *Yes. I have to be myself.*

In the story told, we have seen not only how parents changed their attitudes towards homosexuality, but also how they came to see the possibility of a different future.

The exact features of a society free of homophobia cannot be seen clearly at this time. Our story, however, shows that homophobia can be dropped. As gay people and their families get out from under the burden of the old misconceptions, they want a new relationship not only with each other but with society. They want to be who they are without having to hide, to be labeled, or to be the object of scorn or ridicule. Each person who becomes aware that "gay is okay" and stands up for gay rights, in some way changes society.

Because our parents have changed, we know it is possible for society to change. As we share the images our parents have of new ways of living, we can get a glimpse of a more just and fair society.

Postscript
About Aids

This postscript is dedicated to the memory of Scott Cleaver (1958–1984) and other gay men who have lost their lives from the AIDS virus.

My name is Barbara. My son was diagnosed with AIDS and Kaposi's sarcoma in November of 1983. He died in November of 1984.

We felt lucky because we knew he was gay before we knew he had AIDS. Since he told us he was gay, I had kept up with everything about gay issues. I had read about AIDS and knew what the symptoms were. A friend of my son's called us from San Francisco where he was living, to tell us that Scott was very, very sick. He could barely get out what he was trying to say and when he did, I knew the words Kaposi's sarcoma and what they meant. It was the worst moment for me in the whole thing. Not only did he have AIDS, but he had a bad form of it. He was already very sick and we might lose him soon. And we did. He only lived a year after we found out, and he's been dead a year from last Wednesday. The last two years have been very hard.

At the time of our first interviews, the issue of AIDS seemed very remote. Since AIDS is a new disease, media reports in the early eighties were cautious and limited to incidents on the East and West coasts. It seemed unlikely to our parents that their children might be stricken.

Suddenly the number of cases multiplied exponentially. By 1985, hardly a day went by without media reference—about medical developments, the personal anguish of AIDS patients, or panicky reactions from the public. Our parents' and our own fears moved from the back burner to the foreground of our daily lives. So we felt a need to go back and re-interview a number of parents of gay men. We were interested in finding out how parents who had accepted their childrens' homosexuality were reacting to the scare about AIDS. Their children, who lived in large metropolitan areas, were at risk but had not contracted the disease.

In addition to these parents, we interviewed and collected information from a number of people directly involved with AIDS, including gay men, one of whom had lost a former lover to the disease, and a parent whose son had died from AIDS.

In no way did parents who had moved beyond acceptance reject their child or their child's life style. They searched out new information, looked at their feelings, and made a decision to stand with their children through thick or thin. This is illustrated by the official stand of the Federation of Parents and Friends of Lesbians and Gays, October, 1985:

> Parents are often asked, "What about AIDS?" Our answer is that we love our children in sickness and in health. We shall continue to do all in our power to work for prevention of AIDS and for discovery of a cure. We shall continue to urge that parents give their love and support to all their children. We invite all of society to join us in fighting to overcome fear and hysteria and in responding compassionately to the suffering of patients and their families.[1]

PARENTS WHOSE CHILDREN ARE AT RISK

Those parents who children were at risk found they were confronted with two related problems: the disease itself and the equally serious homophobic reaction to it by the public. All the parents moved in and out of thinking the disease could strike their own child. All were learning to cope with their fears in order to alleviate their sense of helplessness.

Refusal to Be Alarmed

Understandably, our parents reacted to the new threat with defenses to help themselves cope. For all, there have been periods of time when they felt that somehow their children would be protected. This thinking pattern was an effective means for preventing an escalation of fear.

I'm trying to deal with AIDS. I figure my son has one chance in a million of contracting it. He has a greater chance of being killed in an automobile wreck than he has of getting the virus.

Oh, I pray a lot. Deep down I have a gnawing fear, but it is no different than when my kids take a trip on a holiday. I figure that one crazy driver could leave my child dead. So, I'm not panicky about AIDS. I'm just concerned.

I don't worry any more about it than I do about a bunch of macho men saying, "Here's a queer. Let's beat him up." I think people are overreacting to AIDS. The news media has blown the whole thing out of proportion, particularly since Rock Hudson died. I'm afraid it'll be used as an excuse to harass our kids.

Monitoring the Facts As They Emerge

The known facts surrounding AIDS are neither complete at this time, nor are they particularly comforting, but they are much better than rumors and half-knowledge. A major problem is that there is little history of the disease, since it has been on the scene only a few years. Since medical people are increasing their knowledge weekly, we decided not to attempt to review the rapidly changing medical facts. There are many excellent, free and confidential sources of information including local hospitals. Many cities have AIDS hotlines or crisis hotlines which have the most up-to-date information available.

The only thing we know for sure is what AIDS is. "AIDS stands for Acquired Immune Deficiency Syndrome. It causes a breakdown in the body's immune system leaving it vulnerable to infections (especially, PCP, or Pneumocystic carinii pneumonia) and cancers (especially KS, or Kaposi's sarcoma) which normally do not affect healthy people. AIDS is caused by a virus called HTLV-III (Human T-cell Lymphotropic Virus).

There is not yet a cure for AIDS, but treatments for the infections and cancer are available. The virus has been isolated which is the first step in developing a preventive vaccine and a cure."[2]

As of December, 1985, there is a core of reassuring facts about the transmission of AIDS. Dr. Sidney M. Wolfe, director of the Public Citizen Health Research Group, says that the following facts have been so clearly verified that they can be used as the basis for individual and institutional decision making:

> There is no evidence that any of the Americans who have contracted AIDS got the disease from casual contact with another AIDS victim.
>
> Not a single family member of these AIDS victims has caught the disease other than spouses from sexual contact or children born to mothers with AIDS.
>
> Of the tens of thousands of doctors, nurses, or other health workers who have cared for AIDS patients, not a single case of AIDS has developed from patient contact.
>
> The risk to the general public from blood transfusions or blood products for hemophiliacs—about 2 percent of all AIDS cases—has been virtually eliminated by the use of the AIDS antibody screening test for blood.[3]

We can see in the following statement how getting facts helps parents cope.

My son called and said he had a cough and a low-grade fever and that his glands had been swollen. Even though he told us everything had cleared up, I panicked. I went around all week thinking "Oh God, this is it. He has three of the symptoms of AIDS. He's going to die."

At a meeting about AIDS that I attended the following weekend, a doctor said the symptoms had to be persistent for two or three months before they were significant for AIDS. At first I didn't realize that those words had had any impact on my fear. In fact, a day went by before I noticed how much better I felt. I had a sense that we had been spared. I've decided to learn as much as I can about the disease, so that I won't have to go through this kind of pain again.

Reaching Out to Others

There are similarities in the ways parents dealt with the news of gayness and ways they can learn to cope with the fear of AIDS. Reading facts is essential, but parents have to go beyond that and reach out to others—to other parents and to their own children.

As parents explored their situation together, clear thinking and mutual understanding gave them the feeling of being connected with sources of comfort.

I need the group now even more than when I first found out. No one else could possibly understand what I'm feeling. At a recent meeting, we sat and cried and talked over our feelings about AIDS. It was a miserable evening. But I left feeling a whole lot better.

Parents tell us their gay child can be a source of information and reassurance.

Since I found out about Eric's positive antibody test results, I have been trying to get the whole thing into perspective. I don't know why I'm not down more, but I've taken it pretty well. I know there are thousands of cases of AIDS now, but there are hundreds of thousands of cancer cases. I think he may very well not get sick. I'm bothered, but it still hasn't struck me as hard as when he first told me he was gay. I figure life must go on.

Eric's attitude is hopeful, and that helps me a whole lot. He takes care of himself. He gets enough sleep. He doesn't drink or smoke and he tells me he's practicing safe sex.

Devising an Emergency Plan

Many parents seemed to do better if they had a good idea of what they would do if their child had AIDS. Like a fire drill, plans made ahead for a possible emergency can be a source of security.

Sometimes I have the feeling that Tim might get AIDS. I just hope if he gets it, I won't be too old to care for him. I would bring him here to live since I know other people who would help out. He has insurance at his job, so the medical expenses should be taken care of.

Putting Fears on Hold

Once parents had thought through and accepted the possibility that they might have a child with a life-threatening illness, they had to put their fears aside. They chose not to live as though a possibility were a reality.

In the early morning before light, my thoughts are jumbled. They leap from one train of thought to another. I follow them until too much fear forces me away or I feel some measure of comfort.

It's tough right now, but we can handle this. I guess we can handle it. One evening not long ago my son called and said his lymph glands were enlarged. As I listened my head began to ache. By the time I went to bed, my headache was raging, and I felt nauseated. I know my body was telling me of my ongoing fear, though my mind was completely clear.

Still, I have to live as though my child doesn't have AIDS. If he does, there's nothing I can do except be there for him. If he doesn't, then we can go on with our lives.

Parents Helping Others

Besides expressing concerns for their own children, the parents often spoke of ways that they could help those who were suffering from the disease, as well as their families.

I often think, "Just let my son get through this safely." My feelings are all tied up with love, fear, and superstition. We have worked out a good relationship with Chris, where we care very deeply for him, and he seems to care for us. Sometimes, though, I have this superstitious feeling that if you love too much, that person may be taken away from you.

This is a bad time for parents, but I've been through bad times before. What helped? What made things worse? A great way to get depressed is to let your mind concentrate on all the horrible things that could happen. What helped me before was to start doing something. I can write Washington to allow more funds for AIDS research. I can join a work brigade to help persons with AIDS in their homes. Many cities already have parents helping in such brigades. I might be able to console parents whose children have AIDS.

Accepting What We Cannot Change

Always there is a concern for the child, a kind of "feeling with" whatever the parents perceive their child is feeling.

Every time I saw an article about AIDS or heard about it on radio or TV I used to dream about Bob that night. It was always a struggling dream where I'm trying to do something with him, and I can't get it done. One night it seemed like I spent the whole night trying to get him across some town. I tried cars, buses, and trains trying to get him there. But nothing worked.

I had several of these dreams before I connected it with AIDS. I wasn't upset about it, consciously. After I connected it I began to get upset. The more I thought about it the more I decided that Bob fits the model of the type of person likely to get AIDS. He got hepatitis as a teenager, and it seems to me that he's always sick with some minor illness. He's always had long-term relationships but, you never know.

AIDS is something we have to learn to live with. It's just one more thing that we learn to accept. You know, though, if I'm upset about it what do you think Bob is thinking?

Concerns About Homophobia

Beyond the fear of AIDS itself, parents often expressed anger about homophobia. The danger of homophobia is that it draws attention away from the real enemy which is the AIDS virus.

I'm scared about AIDS. I love David. He's a fine, caring human being. His career is just beginning to bloom. He's too young to die.

I want a speedy cure, but I know the odds are against getting one soon. I have to guard myself against false hopes, because the media overreacts to every "cure news" that comes along.

But my fear of the homophobic hatred being whipped up is bigger than my fear of AIDS. It pierces me when I hear some politician "in jest" say "We ought to kill all the queers." There are ambitious demagogues out there who seem to get their jollies by trying to bar gays from jobs, housing and from social acceptance—now even more than they did before. They even try to isolate people who are sick with AIDS. They want to cut them off from the loving care that is at the heart of our religious teachings.

I want the American people to see that homophobia is as destructive a disease for society as AIDS is a physical disease. It can cut us off from the best parts—the justice and equality parts—of our democratic tradition. I want to see that the full civil rights of my son and other gay people are protected in ways that also protect the health of the public.

GAY MEN AT RISK

For gay men, AIDS is not only life threatening on a physical level, but on a psychological level as well. Each gay man is held hostage by the terrible virus. Each has to make adjustments in his life in order to increase his chances of survival. Since no one knows who is infectious and who isn't, it is necessary to operate on the principle that anyone and everyone may be contagious, including themselves.

People in the gay community must combat depression as they learn to live with still another stigma. They face a lessening of support and some reenactment of repressive laws. But lesbians and gay men have risen to the occasion. They have organized in many cities all over the country to help those who have AIDS, to encourage safe sex practices, and to find a cure for the disease. Their response to the crisis sets an example for the entire community.

The following quote was made by a young gay man right after he went through a major scare:

I'm always worried about AIDS, but I keep telling myself that I'm all right and that there is nothing to worry about. The other day I got this rash on my leg and my lymph glands were swollen. I went to the doctor in a panic. He said it wasn't AIDS, just a skin infection of some kind. I felt a little better. I only go to gay doctors. I think they're more likely to be up to date on the latest AIDS information.

I've only been practicing safe sex for the past six or eight months. What this means for me is that I just don't have sex anymore. I'm putting all my energies into my job instead. My lover and I stay ten feet apart and hold hands.

Another gay man was willing to share with us his experiences as he went through losing someone he loved. Ted and Leon were lovers for two and one-half years. They remained close friends even after their relationship ended. Leon contracted AIDS about three years after the breakup. From the onset of the disease until his death three years later, Ted was very much on the scene since Leon was alienated from his mother and father.

Initially, the anxiety of not knowing what was wrong was the hardest part of what we went through. This was early in the time that AIDS was coming on the scene. Leon was very sick in the spring of 1982, but the testing was not definitive at that time. We were living with a time bomb—did he have AIDS or was it just a bad scare? The uncertainty and ambiguousness were extremely hard for us to deal with. It was some time before we knew for sure.

There are many hard parts about losing someone you love to AIDS. One of the hardest is seeing him suffer and decline, and knowing there is little you can do to stop it. You can only bring a more peaceful, loving attitude into the relationship, but you can't control the outcome.

There were other difficult parts: the financial problems, the problems of a loss of energy, the depression, the boredom, the isolation, the discrimination. Leon almost lost his job. He had to get a lawyer and confront his employer. It's not unusual for people to be kicked out of their jobs and houses.

But Leon had a network of people who ministered to his needs. It wasn't just me. There were all those wonderful men and women who helped. So even though there was anxiety, there was also a developing sense of freedom and a feeling of growing up. People found that it was good to give services and help. Leon himself said that the last year of his life was one of his happiest since he was surrounded by so much caring and help. I've worked through much of my grief now, and I see my life as being richer and deeper. I'm thinking of having a baby, and I've let go of some old patterns of dependency. I'm doing things I might have put off. The threat of AIDS has left me with a new directive—live now, grow now.

Sharing Leon's experience and my own work as a clinical psychologist has shown me how disorienting the whole issue can be. The sexual needs of the person with AIDS are a major problem. Where does he go with them? He may feel rejected. His body is less and less attractive. This may be a great loss. So for vanity and energy reasons, people with AIDS often isolate themselves.

Then there's the family. They have to decide whether to tell their parents at all, whether to tell them part of the truth, or to tell them everything. What do you say if you have only six more months to live? There can be a feeling of failure that they haven't handled the family right or a fear of the ultimate rejection. Some lie because they just don't want to deal with their family's shock.

There is a double stigma, against being gay and also having AIDS. If the person with AIDS feels guilty about being gay, this can lead to depression and self-hate. It can increase to the extent that the sick person may abandon any attempts to get medical care or take care of himself.

Though it's hard to speak about without sounding moralistic, there is a self-loving, affirmative part that's developing in gay men as a result of this crisis. Many are going for more depth and less breadth in their relationships. There is more intimacy and monogamy. This isn't developing by leaps and bounds, but it is developing.

Really it's your old paradox: pain, confusion, insecurity, and inadequacy can lead to more growth, strength, caring for the self, and caring more for others.

A MOTHER WHOSE SON DIED FROM AIDS

Barbara Cleaver, whose words opened this chapter, tells us of the suffering she and her son endured as he was dying.

Scott lived in San Francisco, and we lived in L.A. That whole year my phone bill was astronomical. When I first found out how sick he was, I had no one to turn to. I needed to talk and most of the time felt moderately hysterical. My husband holds his feelings inside and didn't need to talk. He and I did not share much about our feelings for eleven of the twelve months that we dealt with Scott's illness. But in the last month we turned toward each other and were close again.

I went into the whole thing armed with no knowledge. I did take a course in death and dying at the local junior college which helped some. Of course I couldn't tell them that my son had AIDS. That meant I didn't get as much help as people whose loved ones had more "acceptable" diseases.

I kept pushing and pushing to get through it. I couldn't come out at work and tell anyone. I'm a hairdresser, and I work in a conservative area. The people are wealthy and wouldn't allow a mother who has contact with a son with AIDS to work there. I had to keep quiet. But somehow I kept functioning. I never missed a day until three weeks before Scott died. But the whole time I was experiencing a quiet hysteria. I drank wine every night, took pain pills, and cried alone. I felt like I was two people, one who was going about her usual life and one who was in a desperate and debilitating state of grief. The stigma that goes with AIDS separated me from most support systems.

Scott was the one who helped me the most. He and I went through it together. He went about dealing with the disease in a businesslike manner. He took care of his affairs, quit his job, went on disability, became a part of a speaker's bureau, and found ways he could help others who had the disease. He participated in support groups and discovered square dancing.

We wanted him home in Los Angeles with us, but we knew he was receiving excellent care and treatment at San Francisco General Hospital. We knew he would not choose to come back here. San Francisco was his home and his community.

As the year went on, I found myself gathering strength from Scott. He advised me to act as a volunteer for a group in L.A. who were helping people with AIDS. I was never afraid of the disease for myself, and I began volunteering my hair-cutting skills for AIDS patients. I met bright, courageous, witty men, all fighting for their lives. I met men bogged down with paperwork, longing for understanding, some with no family support at all. A common thread bound us all together— hope.

Some of those men became my friends. Six of them died that year. Somehow that work helped me. As I grieved for each of them, I learned how to grieve for my son. Later, though, as Scott got sicker I found out that I couldn't continue to be with people who were so close to death. It brought the reality of Scott's impending death too close, and I was having a hard time going on. Instead, I joined the speaker's bureau and went around and talked about having a son with AIDS. I think I was able to do some good.

My second worst moment was Scott's diagnosis of pneumocystic pneumonia five months before his death. I felt devastated that day in the hospital. For a short time I lost all ground emotionally, and I felt like I had back at the beginning. But he got through that crisis and I got myself back on track. On the day that he got out of the hospital, he rode and I walked beside him in the Gay Pride Parade in his city.

I had one friend who was particularly helpful. She, like Scott, gave me strength. She was a member of AA and understood what it was like to have an illness that has stigma with it. She was very helpful to me spiritually and turned me towards God.

My mother was another source of help because she understood so much of what Scott was feeling. She was with us all the way through. She had had tuberculosis when she was in her twenties. She knew how it felt to have an illness that was considered fatal and that no one was sure how it was transmitted. At the time she had TB, people felt towards it like they do towards AIDS now. People didn't visit her, and while she was in the hospital they came in with masks and gloves.

His friends were also a lot of help. They surrounded Scott and my husband and me with love and understanding. They helped out with his physical care. They visited often and were with us at the end.

Three weeks before Scott died, I went to stay with him. He didn't want to go back into a hospital. He wanted to stay in his apartment. I encountered some things I wasn't prepared for: his disorientation about where he was, hallucinations, hours turned upside down, and a constant preoccupation with his medications. I would be cheerful when I was with him and then go into another room and cry.

It was hard. I called a local hospice, but there was nobody who could come in and help me bathe him and help with all the problems I had with his diarrhea. I did twenty-four-hour-a-day duty with a bare *minimum of help. When someone came to relieve me I walked and cried as fast and as hard as I could.*

Someone told me during these weeks that I should tell him it was okay to let go. I felt unsure about saying that to him, but I wanted to do everything I could to make it easier for Scott. So, I told him. I don't think it was a good idea. He seemed upset afterward. I decided that I should have listened to my own instincts.

It was the worst of times for me, but somehow it was also the best. I wouldn't have missed that time alone with him for the world. During the hard times I could hold him and help him. During the easier times I'd rub his back. Sometimes he'd even rub mine. We were very close. Any parents who would reject their child because of AIDS are missing a time of closeness that can be very beautiful.

Ten days before Scott died, we visited the clinic. His doctor told him, with me present, that they could do no more with treatments, and wanted him to be comfortable and have all the medication he wanted. I heard myself thank him. We literally carried Scott out of the hospital and home. That same man made a house call in the rain a few days later.

The last five days my husband and daughter came up and were with us. Now the whole family was together. The hospice came through and sent in a nurse who helped with the medicine and bathing. My son was one of the lucky ones, surrounded by friends and family—people who loved him and truly cared. We all vowed to keep him at home, and we did exactly that.

God and Scott ran the whole show. We did whatever Scott wanted. I think people who love someone who is terminally ill should let them do it their way. We need to be as loving and supportive as we can, but the person who is ill should make the major decisions. Scott did, and I feel good about that.

Several people were with us that last day. At one point, my husband and I needed some air. We went out to the Conservatory of Flowers. While we were gone, Scott died. A friend was with him when he took his last breath. It was a friend who was quiet and strong and just the person to be with him. Scott had a picture above his bed from the Conservatory of Flowers. Somehow I felt that God helped us by sending us to a place that Scott loved so much. That kept us connected during that last moment in a way that was good for everyone.

When my husband and I got back, everyone went into his bedroom. We sat on the bed with Scott for a good while. Everyone shared his death. Then we made hamburgers and bought champagne. I felt lucky to be a part of all the people who loved Scott. I felt wrapped in love and the Supreme Being.

Sometimes when I think of not going up to take care of him the whole last year instead of the last three weeks, I feel guilty. But Scott had a saying in his room that I now have with me: "P.S. I have no regrets."

I'm still having trouble being completely open about having had a son with AIDS. Eventually I will be. I feel horrible about this dishonesty. Somehow his whole humanity is at stake when I have to hide. I feel anger over the unreasonable fear that I always hear about AIDS. In fact, sometimes I feel like I'm just a mixture of anger and sadness. Right now I'm very hostile and defensive. I don't like this feeling, and I'm working on changing it, but I assume that a person is prejudiced and bigoted until I know differently. I go around and talk to groups who are supportive. Every time I do, I feel a bit better. I want to help someone else and that helps me.

I'm just now beginning to feel that I have the right to feel good again. I know Scott wouldn't want me to feel bad the rest of my life. I've taken up aerobics again. Scott would be happy if he knew I was going on with my life. He always wanted the best for me.

The night before the anniversary of Scott's death was very hard. But on the anniversary itself, the whole family went to an amusement park and had a good time. We had a celebration of Scott's life with us. Our family is stronger. Even with one member physically missing, we're spiritually closer. The precious gifts he left with us will remain forever.

NOTES FOR POSTSCRIPT

[1]Resolution passed by Board of Directors of Federation of Parents and Friends of Lesbians and Gays (Parents FLAG), October 28, 1985.

[2]"What is AIDS?" *The Acquired Immune Deficiency Syndrome,* AIDS Atlanta (1985).

[3]Dr. Sidney M. Wolfe, "AIDS Hysteria," *Public Citizen* (December 1985) pp. 20-21.

Afterword from G. M. Griffin*

Often I think children of a certain age are so involved in becoming adults and establishing their own lives, that they neglect to consider the changes and growth, love and support of their families. I plead guilty to the above and thus I am grateful to have been given this opportunity to remark about two rather extraordinary people, my mom and dad.

I struggled, cried, and despaired about my own emerging sexuality from before I was twelve years old until I was almost eighteen. At that point, while still in high school, I rather grandiosely informed my parents that I was a homosexual and dating a man eighteen years my senior. That was a very difficult decision for me, but somehow in my naiveté, or rather innocence, I thought that having told them the "facts" of the matter, the issues would immediately be resolved. It took much longer. I ignored the time that it took me to come to the first steps of accepting myself. I ignored my parents' expectations of grandchildren and the traditional extended familial relationships that they were anticipating. But I did not forget how much they loved me—a fact that probably made things more difficult for them.

I never doubted my parents. I never thought for a minute they would cut off our relationship. I never thought that they would not come to respect and understand me as a gay man. And they have.

There is a lot of lip service paid these days to family values. Many associate these values—love, support, loyalty, integrity, morality, stability—only with traditional families. These values need no defense, nor does the traditional family. But an alternative family or life style does not preclude having those values. I'm pretty lucky in this area with my own family.

---

*G. M. Griffin, Ph.D., is a mathematical psychologist.

I think this book may bring families closer together, and maybe even make a real difference in some people's lives. I hope knowing this gives my mom and dad the joy and pride they deserve. Thanks, Mom and Dad.

*Afterword from Scott Wirth**

For the gay nature which lay behind the vision and trouble that bore this book, I give thanks. To my mother and father, for their journey and for their love, I give thanks.

My parents and I took the opportunity to make the truth of who we were the priority of our adult relationship. In opening ourselves we have come to see and largely heal the rifts that separated us in the years of my childhood and adolescence.

Gay people may recognize the sources of such missed connections: A young father's need for his son to be an image of himself that the son does not fulfill; then the wounded son's withdrawal from the disappointed father; a mother's sensing her son as "different," and encouraging him to be so in the "safer" ways—"He is musical." She shrinks back from her intuitions about him in order to be an "appropriate" mother. Both parents become fascinated and bewildered by their son's "sensitivity," by his disregard for gender-typed interests, by their own feelings that there is something indefinably "wrong" about themselves or him, by their feelings of being depressed, mute, or angry. This son, as a teenager, numbing his sexual being for lack of role models or validation; finding no approving gleam in his parents' eyes, and no response from his peers' experiences.

He and they cannot sort out whether the "differentness" lies in his true self or in his "problems." What is this differentness anyhow? "It" is vague, a threatening whisper in the mind, not to be reinforced. Out of the helplessness of not knowing, come the clichés: "It will pass—it's just a phase—he's sensitive—we do the best we can." Even living beneath the same roof, they inadvertently misconstrue each other.

---

*Scott Wirth, Ph.D., is a psychologist and consultant in private practice in San Francisco, California.

But this misunderstanding was not simply an isolated family matter. There was no room in society for gay and lesbian children or youth. The McCarthyist society of the fifties and early sixties was systematically hostile to racial and ethnic minorities, women, and political dissidents as well as to gay people—in fact, to anyone other than prosperous heterosexual white males.

Beyond Acceptance makes it plain that adult gay children and their parents need not protect each other from telling their stories. Raising my parents' consciousness also meant sensitizing them—to themselves, to each other, to "modern times." In the early stages, this effort felt burdensome to me. I felt that I shouldn't have had to do all that work. At different times I felt indignant, trapped, resigned, or lost for having to, in a sense, parent my parents.

Yet, what once seemed an undue imposition has evolved into a mutual process of joyful struggle and deepening intimacy. This newfound honesty led us not only back to each other, but out into the world of human service—for myself as a psychologist and community activist—for my parents as authors and Parents FLAG organizers.

Service often comes best out of work on ourselves. And in this work on ourselves, as is said in Zen, "the greater the hindrance, the greater the enlightenment." Sharing this philosophy with each other, we came to know our "enlightenment" as a process that includes setbacks. There is an inevitable return to the edge of frustration or discouragement. Whatever that edge may be, we can meet it with patience. That patience will see us through our resistance to change.

For some parents, growth may mean going beyond a virtuous or martyred I-accept-my-child stance. For some lesbians and gay men, personal growth may mean accepting the nonacceptance of parents and siblings and finding a self-love within. Whether we are challenging and confronting, or letting go and letting be, what seems needed is an openness to the unexpected.

Gayness or lesbianism presents itself in our lives unexpectedly. It goes on to surprise us, to confuse us, to disappear and reappear, to open us. Just about the time we think we truly affirm the dignity of gay people, we may feel like Judas Iscariot as we let an ignorant comment or joke breeze through a conversation. Just as we find our comfortable orientation number on the Kinsey scale, we experience feelings or fantasies at the other end of the spectrum. Right after a lecture against stereotypes of gay people, someone walks in who seems to fit them all. Grandchildren may be born to the lesbian daughter or gay son for whom a parent had ruled out the possibility. Reading a shelf of books about the origins of sexual orientation, we are reduced to a two-syllable conclusion: "Don't know." After working through our phobic attitudes about the sexual part of homosexuality, we hear that gay people resent an overemphasis on sex in gay relationships. The very designation "gay" may seem a liberating affirmation of identity in one moment, then a simple, utterly dehumanizing label in the next.

Being gay, or closely related to someone who is, offers an uncommonly powerful catalyst for personal transformation. If we can stand the heat and give ourselves over to the full scope of the process of coming out, we will learn flexibility in the midst of life's chaos, paradox, and mystery.

Appendix

Parents and Friends of Lesbians and Gays (Parents FLAG) is a nonsectarian, nonprofit, all-volunteer organization. Its purpose is to help parents so that they can help themselves and their gay or lesbian children.

Parents FLAG is represented in almost every state by one or more groups, or by "contacts" (that is, parents or friends operating as helpers without a group). For more information, call or write the regional headquarters nearest you. Each has a national directory. You also may contact the national headquarters located in Los Angeles.

Two additional sources of information are: the nearest gay and lesbian hot line, or a local branch of the Metropolitan Community Church, which serves gay people.

Be persistent. Telephone and box numbers change over time, but the network is large enough for you to make contact. We know from our own experience that your persistence will be rewarded.

ATLANTIC SOUTHERN REGION: Delaware, District of Columbia, Florida, Georgia, Maryland, North Carolina, South Carolina, Virginia, West Virginia.

Regional Headquarters: Ft. Lauderdale-Broward County, Florida, Parents FLAG, P.O. Box 16682, Plantation, FL 33318. (305) 741-3648.

District of Columbia, Maryland, and Virginia: Parents FLAG of the Washington Metro Area, P.O. Box 3533, Silver Spring, MD 20901. (301) 439-FLAG; (301) 587-5242; (301) 652-7975.

SOUTHERN REGION: Alabama, Arkansas, Louisiana, Mississippi, Oklahoma, Texas.

Regional Headquarters: New Orleans PFG, P.O. Box 15515, New Orleans, LA 70175. (504) 891-3866.

CENTRAL REGION: Illinois, Indiana, Iowa, Kentucky, Michigan, Minnesota, Missouri, Ohio, Tennessee, Wisconsin.

Regional Headquarters: Greater St. Louis Parents FLAG, 7443 Cromwell Dr., St. Louis, MO 63105, (314) 863-2748, or 114 Westridge, Collinsville, IL 62234, (618) 344-7765.

Akron, Ohio: Akron Parents FLAG, P.O. Box 6146, Akron, OH 44312. (216) 794-9623.

MOUNTAINS–PLAINS REGION: Colorado, Kansas, Nebraska, New Mexico, North Dakota, South Dakota, Wyoming.

Regional Headquarters: Denver Parents FLAG, P.O. Box 18901, Denver, CO 80218. (303) 333-0286.

NEW YORK CITY REGION: New York City Parents FLAG, P.O. Box 553, Lenox Hill Station, New York, NY 10021. (914) 793-5198.

NORTHEAST REGION: East Canada, New England, New Jersey, New York State, Pennsylvania.

Regional Headquarters: Buffalo Relatives and Friends of Gays and Lesbians, c/o Child-Family Services, 330 Delaware Avenue, Buffalo, NY 14202. (716) 627-2402.

Philadelphia, Pennsylvania: Philadelphia Parents FLAG, P.O. Box 15711, Philadelphia, PA 19103. (215) 848-7071; (215) 572-1833.

PACIFIC NORTHWEST REGION: Alaska, Idaho, Montana, Oregon, Utah, Washington, West Canada.

Regional Headquarters: Portland Parents FLAG, P.O. Box 230266, Portland, OR 97223. (503) 639-5609; (503) 252-7886; (503) 244-3225; (503) 256-5654.

Seattle, Washington: Seattle Parents FLAG, 2432-63rd St. S.E.,Mercer Island, WA 98040. (206) 325-3813 (days); (206) 282-5004 (evenings).

PACIFIC SOUTHWEST REGION: Arizona, California, Nevada, Hawaii.

Regional Headquarters: Sacramento Parents FLAG, P.O. Box 660955, Sacramento, CA 95866. (916) 443-5710.

San Francisco, California: Parents FLAG, P.O. Box 640223, San Francisco, CA 94164. (415) 928-2748; (415) 347-7958; (415) 668-2128.

Phoenix, Arizona: Parents FLAG, P.O. Box 37525, Phoenix, AZ 85069. (602) 939-7807; (602) 946-1024.

LOS ANGELES REGION AND NATIONAL HEADQUARTERS: Los Angeles Parents FLAG, P.O. Box 24565, Los Angeles, CA 90024. (213) 472-8952; (818) 995-3647; (213) 395-4495.

Bibliography

WORKS CITED IN THE TEXT

Bartlett, John, *Familiar Quotations.* Boston: Little, Brown and Co., 1980.

Bell, Alan P., Martin S. Weinberg, and Sue K. Hammersmith, *Sexual Preference: Its Development in Men and Women.* Bloomington: Indiana University Press, 1981.

Bieber, Irving et al., eds., *Homosexuality: A Psychoanalytic Study.* New York: Basic Books, 1962.

Brown, Howard, *Familiar Faces, Hidden Lives: The Story of Homosexual Men in America Today.* New York: Harcourt Brace Jovanovich, 1976.

Czillinger, Rev. Kenneth, *Newsletter,* American Association of Retired People (March 1983).

Freedman, Mark, "Stimulus-Response: Homosexuals May Be Healthier Than Straights," *Psychology Today,* 8, no. 10 (March 1975) 28–32.

Gantz, Joe, *Whose Child Cries: Children of Gay Parents Talk About Their Lives.* Rolling Hills Estates, CA: Jalmar Press, 1983.

Hooker, Evelyn, "The Adjustment of the Male Overt Homosexual," *Journal of Projective Techniques,* 21, no. 1 (1957) 17–31.

Kinsey, Alfred C. et al., *Sexual Behavior in the Human Female.* Philadelphia: W.B. Saunders Co., 1953.

Kinsey, Alfred C., Wardell B. Pomeroy and Clyde E. Martin, *Sexual Behavior in the Human Male.* Philadelphia: W. B. Saunders Co., 1948.

Koertge, Noretta, ed., *Nature and Causes of Homosexuality: A Philosophic and Scientific Inquiry.* New York: The Haworth Press, 1982.

Masters, W. H., and V. E. Johnson, *Homosexuality in Perspective.* Boston: Little, Brown and Co., 1979.

Near, Holly, comp., "Unity," *Journeys* record album. Oakland, CA: Redwood Records.

Nelson, James B., *Embodiment: An Approach to Sexuality and Christian Theology.* New York: Pilgrim Press, 1978.

191

Nugent, Robert, Jeannine Gramick and Thomas Oddo, *Homosexual Catholics: A New Primer for Discussion.* Washington, DC: Dignity, Inc., 1980.

O'Shea, Kevin, *Dignity Newsletter,* 3, no. 3 (April 1, 1983).

Paul, William et al., eds., *Homosexuality: Social, Psychological and Biological Issues.* Beverly Hills, CA: Sage Publications, Inc., 1982.

Pittenger, Norman, *Time for Consent: A Christian's Approach to Homosexuality.* London: SCM Press, Ltd., 1976.

Scanzoni, Letha Dawson, "Putting a Face on Homosexuality," *The Other Side,* Issue 149 (February 1984) pp. 8–10.

Scanzoni, Letha, and Virginia Ramey Mollenkott, *Is the Homosexual My Neighbor?* San Francisco: Harper and Row, 1978.

Starr, Adele, statement in *About Our Children,* Los Angeles: Federation of Parents and Friends of Lesbians and Gays, Inc., 1978. Pamphlet available free, Box 24565, Los Angeles, CA 90024.

Towards a Quaker View of Sex: An Essay by a Group of Friends. London: Friends House, 1963.

"What Is Aids?" *The Acquired Immune Deficiency Syndrome,* AIDS Atlanta (1985).

Wolfe, Dr. Sidney M., "AIDS Hysteria," *Public Citizen* (December 1985) pp. 20–21.

ADDITIONAL WORKS

Back, Gloria W., *Are You Still My Mother? Are You Still My Family?* New York: Warner Books, 1985.

Berzon, Betty, and Robert Leighton, eds., *Positively Gay.* Millbrae, CA: Celestial Arts, 1979.

Borhek, Mary V., *Coming Out to Parents: A Two-Way Survival Guide for Lesbians and Gay Men and Their Parents.* New York: The Pilgrim Press, 1983.

Borhek, Mary V., *My Son Eric.* New York: The Pilgrim Press, 1979.

Clark, Don, *Loving Someone Gay.* Millbrae, CA: Celestial Arts, 1977.

Fairchild, Betty, and Nancy Hayward, *Now That You Know: What Every Parent Should Know About Homosexuality.* New York: Harcourt Brace Jovanovich, 1979. Highly recommended.

Heron, Ann, *One Teenager in Ten: Writings by Gay and Lesbian Youth.* Boston: Alyson Publications, Inc., 1983.

Hobson, Laura F., *Consenting Adult.* New York: Warner Books, 1975. Fictional account of a family's struggle.

Katz, Jonathan, *Gay American History: Lesbians and Gay Men in the U.S.A.* New York: Thomas Y. Crowell Co., 1976.

Martin, Del, and Phyllis Lyon, *Lesbian/Woman.* New York: Bantam Books, 1977.

McNaught, Brian, *A Disturbed Peace: Selected Writings of an Irish Catholic Homosexual.* Washington, DC: Dignity, Inc., 1981. Dispels the myth that gays give up morals and religion.

McWhirter, David P., and Andrew M. Mattison, *The Male Couple: How Relationships Develop.* Englewood Cliffs, NJ: Prentice-Hall, Inc., 1984. An account of long-term relationships.

Nugent, Robert, *A Challenge to Love: Gay and Lesbian Catholics in the Church.* New York: Crossroad, 1983.

Pennington, Sylvia, *But Lord, They're Gay.* Hawthorne, CA: Lambda Christian Fellowship, 1981. Helpful to people concerned about the Bible.

Pogrebin, Letty Cottin, *Growing Up Free: Raising Your Child in the 80's.* New York: McGraw-Hill, 1980. On how not to be a homophobic parent.

Tripp, C. A., *The Homosexual Matrix.* New York: New American Library, 1975. A classic with a scientific slant.

Weinberg, George, *Society and the Healthy Homosexual.* New York: St. Martin's Press, 1972. Deals with the myth of the "sick" homosexual.

Wirth, Scott A., "Coming Out Close to Home," *Catalyst,* no. 3 (1978) pp. 6–22.

Index